A FARMER'S ALPHABET

MARY AZARIAN

DAVID R. GODINE✚PUBLISHER
✚BOSTON✚

First published in 1981 by
David R. Godine, Publisher, Inc.
306 Dartmouth Street
Boston, Massachusetts 02116

Copyright © 1981 by Mary Azarian

ISBN 0-87923-394-X (hardcover)
ISBN 0-87923-397-4 (softcover)
LC 80-84938

Designed by Hal Morgan

Fourth printing, November 1982

Printed in the United States of America

Dd

Dog

Ee

Eggs

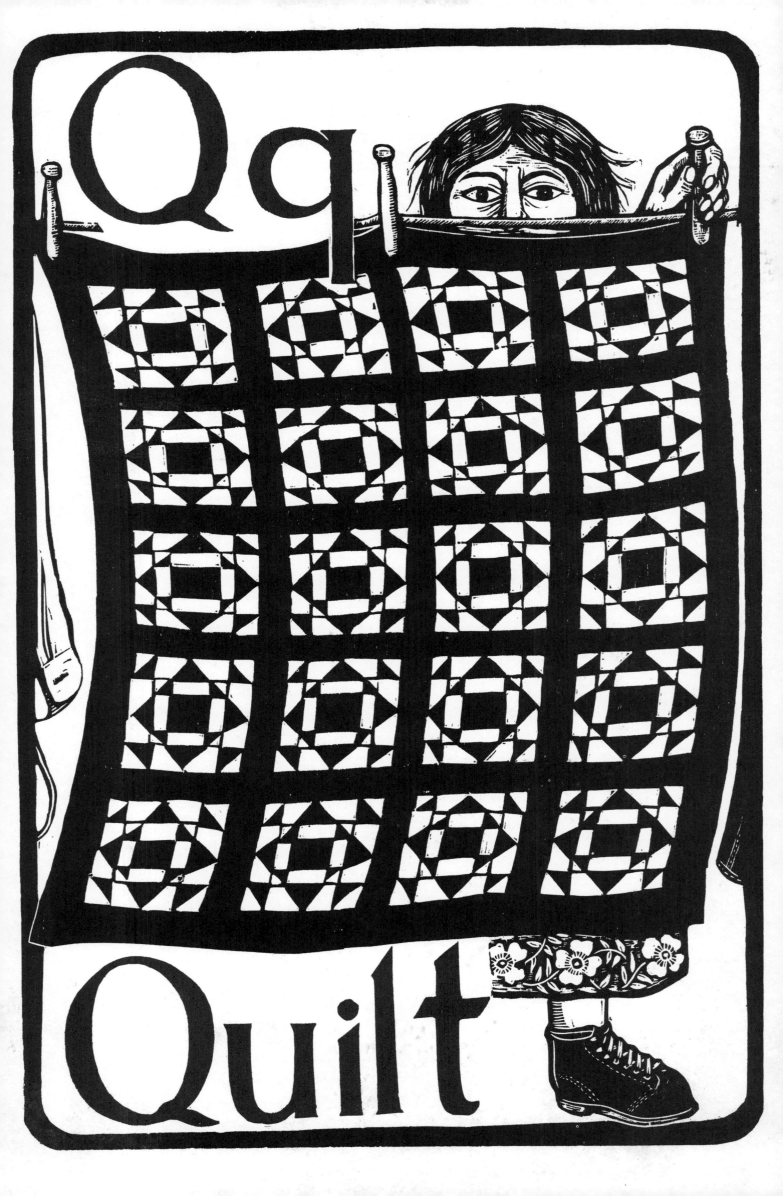

Rr

Rocker

S s

Stove

Uu

OUR GLENWOOD

Underwear

Zz

Zinnia

Artist's Note

THE IDEA of doing an alphabet related to rural themes grew during my years as a teacher in a one-room school in northern Vermont. Arriving for my first day of teaching, I found the large schoolroom entirely bare, except for the wooden desks. An inspection of the various cupboards and shelves revealed only a scattering of old textbooks. The need for warmth, light, and color was obvious, and my first project was to make a set of alphabet posters that almost encircled the room. This was the beginning of a fascination with alphabet images that has stayed with me long after my teaching days ended.

I began designing *A Farmer's Alphabet* with the idea of creating a decorative teaching aid that would celebrate some of the rural traditions that still are observed in New England today. I grew up on a small Virginia farm and watched while it and the surrounding countryside were slowly flattened into an asphalt suburbia, a depressing process to observe and one that is being repeated across rural America at an ever-quickening pace. I wanted to make an alphabet to replace the many urban-oriented ones already available, and thus help in the fight to maintain regional diversity. The idea of hundreds of farm and village children learning that "M is for MacDonalds" or "S is for Shopping Mall," and that such signs of "progress" are both desirable and inevitable, dismayed me. It is sad that traditions are valued only after they are lost. In my own alphabet, "M" would be for "Maple Syrup," in recognition of an important springtime activity on many small farms, and "S" would be represented by "Stove," one of those big black woodburning cookstoves that still warm many rural kitchens. In choosing each image, I tried to avoid quaintness and concentrated instead on activities or objects of proven practicality and relevance to modern life. Fortunately, Vermont's Department of Education approved of my plans and decided to have enough sets printed to supply every elementary school in Vermont.

Each alphabet poster was done as a woodcut. The woodcut is one of the old-est methods of making a picture that can be reproduced many times. It is a simple craft, requiring only a piece of suitable wood, a set of good quality woodcut knives, ink, and paper on which to print the finished carving. A design is drawn directly onto a piece of smooth straight-grained wood, and one must always remember that the printed image will be the reverse of the drawing on the block. Letters must be carefully drawn backwards or the printed words will be unreadable.

THIS IS
BACKWARDS

After the drawing is completed, all areas of the wood block *not drawn on* are

cut away, leaving the original image in the form of raised ridges. The block is then inked with a roller, or brayer, and a piece of special handmade rice paper is carefully laid on the inked block. The woodcut is printed by rubbing on the paper with a smooth wooden dowel or a wooden spoon. This transfers the image from the block to the paper. It is essential not to move the paper while printing or the printed image will be distorted. The finished print is then hung up to dry for a day or so. Many prints can be made from one block, and presses are sometimes used to print woodcuts in larger quantities.

Every artist has his or her own favorite medium of work. Although I have done both painting and drawing, woodcutting remains for me the most exciting form of expression. I occasionally work in maple or cherry, but prefer basswood, some of which comes from the woodlot of our hillside farm. I feel very fortunate to have been able to make a profession of doing woodcuts in a still beautiful rural area.

A FARMER'S ALPHABET
has been set in Cheltenham Old Style by Typographic House of
Boston, Massachusetts. The Cheltenham family of faces,
designed by Bertram G. Goodhue for Ingalls Kimball of the
Cheltenham Press of New York, was offered in the catalogues of
the American Type Founders in twelve variations.
An immediate success, it combined the obvious virtues of
legibility and printability with overtones of Art Nouveau and
William Morris. In the first twenty years of this century
Cheltenham was used more widely for both book and advertising
work than any other type in America. The paper is
Monadnock Text, an entirely acid-free laid sheet. The book
has been printed offset and bound by Book Press
of Brattleboro, Vermont.

Vocabu-Lit

Reading Your Way to Word Power

F A L C O N

Table of Contents

Using the *Vocabu-Lit* Program

Vocabu-Lit is a unique vocabulary program. In format and approach, it differs in several ways from the usual vocabulary-building materials.

First, *Vocabu-Lit* contains examples of how the vocabulary words have been used by various writers and speakers. Reading the different passages not only will expose you to good writing but also will show you how vocabulary can become an effective writing tool.

Second, *Vocabu-Lit* does not ask you to learn a large number of words at one sitting. Instead, you work with just ten words at a time and are provided several experiences with those words. Each experience reinforces the previous one, helping you to master meaning.

Third, *Vocabu-Lit* takes advantage of the way you naturally acquire language by having you study words in context. Learning words through context aids you in two ways. First, it leads you to define a word more precisely. It also helps you develop an important reading skill: the ability to use clues from surrounding words and sentences to determine a word's meaning.

Reading the Passage

Each lesson begins with a selection from a book, essay, story, poem, or speech. You are encouraged to read straight through the selection without paying particular attention to the Master Words (the ten words in dark type). Your understanding of the general meaning of the passage should help you determine the definitions of the Master Words. Then you are advised to read the passage again, this time paying closer attention to the Master Words.

Self-testing for Understanding

The first exercise is a self-test. It will help you identify the words which you have not yet mastered. Often you may think you know a Master Word. But the meaning you know may differ from the meaning of the word as it is used in the passage. Or you may be unable to state the exact definition of a word. This exercise teaches you to look at a word in context and define its meaning more precisely.

To examine a word in context, you can study the surrounding words and sentences. For example, "He was a *mendicant* because he had to beg." Using the context "because he had to beg," you may be able to tell that a mendicant is a beggar. Other times, opposite or contrasting terms may reveal the meaning: "He was far from poor; in fact, he was *affluent*." Obviously, in this context, *affluent* means "rich." Sometimes an unfamiliar word may be followed by examples which explain it, as in "Mrs. Murphy was a *hospitable* woman who warmly welcomed her son's friends." Key words such as *means, is, for example, in other words,* or *and so forth* may help determine a word's meaning.

Note: In some cases, the form of the Master Word in the self-test is not the same as in the passage. Generally, these changes were made to provide you with a more commonly used form of the word.

Writing Definitions

In the second exercise, you are asked to write definitions of the Master Words. The first part of the exercise asks that you define as many of the ten words as you can without using a dictionary. You should use context clues from the passage and any previous experience you may have had with the words to write your definitions.

The second part of the exercise asks you to look up each word in a dictionary and copy an appropriate definition in the space provided. You may wish to compare this definition to your definition.

Note: The part of speech of the words as they will be used in the *exercises* is already indicated in the exercise. This may be different from the words' function in the passage, but you may still find it helpful to look for clues in the surrounding words or sentences.

Choosing Synonyms and Antonyms

This exercise asks you to pick a synonym and antonym for each Master Word. A synonym is a word that means *nearly the same* as another; an antonym is a word that means *nearly the opposite.*

Since you may not be familiar with all the words in the list of synonyms and antonyms, you may find it useful to keep a dictionary handy.

Note: There are no appropriate antonyms for some Master Words. In such cases, the antonym blank has been marked with an X. Also, a synonym or antonym may seem to match more than one Master Word in the exercise. Try to choose the word that is the best synonym or antonym for each Master Word.

Completing Analogies

In the fourth exercise, you are asked to complete word analogies using the Master Words. (An analogy is a comparison between two or more related things.) Again, you will be working with synonyms and antonyms (though different from those in the third exercise).

This exercise contains two types of analogies—words expressing *similar* relationships and words expressing *opposite* relationships. Look at the following example.

day :night ::rich :_____

The symbol **:** means "is to" and **::** means "as." Thus, the analogy could be read "Day is to night as rich is to _____."
· The words *day* and *night* are opposites, or antonyms. So you should look for an antonym of *rich* in your list of Master Words. The Master Word *penniless* would be a correct response.

Fitting Words into Context

The next exercise includes ten sentences. You are to complete each sentence with the appropriate Master Word. Each sentence supplies clues to help you select the best answer. Thus, while testing your understanding of the new words, this exercise also provides practice for using the Master Words in context.

Playing with the Words

In the final exercise, you use the Master Words to solve a variety of puzzles. Traditional games such as acrostics, crosswords, and word spirals are offered. But there are also more unusual puzzles that challenge you to arrange words by degree, play associations, and complete word fact tables. Another word game asks you to invent definitions for words which have been created by joining parts of the Master Words. You are even invited to write stories using some of your newly acquired vocabulary.

Reviewing Knowledge

There are three review lessons in every *Vocabu-Lit* (Lessons 12, 24, and 36). These lessons test your mastery of the vocabulary words from the previous eleven lessons by having you complete more sentences and analogies.

LESSON 1

Read the following selection to get the general meaning. Read it a second time, paying special attention to the words in dark type. Notice how they are used in sentences. These are Master Words. These are the words you will be working with in this lesson.

From "The Bottle Imp"
by Robert Louis Stevenson

"This is the bottle," said the man; and, when Keawe laughed, "You do not believe me?" he added. "Try, then, for yourself. See if you can break it."

So Keawe took the bottle up and **dashed** it on the floor till he was weary; but it jumped on the floor like a child's ball, and was not injured.

"This is a strange thing," said Keawe. "For by the touch of it, as well as by the look, the bottle should be of glass."

"Of glass it is," replied the man, sighing more heavily than ever; "but the glass of it was **tempered** in the flames of hell. An **imp** lives in it, and that is the shadow we behold there moving; or, so I suppose. If any man buy this bottle the imp is at his command; all that he desires—love, fame, money, houses like this house, ay, or a city like this city—all are his at the word **uttered.** Napoleon had this bottle, and by it he grew to be the king of the world; but he sold it at the last and fell. Captain Cook had this bottle, and by it he found his way to so many islands; but he, too, sold it, and was **slain** upon Hawaii. For, once it is sold, the power goes and the protection; and unless a man remain content with what he has, ill will befall him."

"And yet you talk of selling it yourself?" Keawe said.

"I have all I wish, and I am growing elderly," replied the man. "There is one thing the imp cannot do—he cannot **prolong** life; and, it would not be fair to **conceal** from you there is a **drawback** to the bottle; for if a man die before he sells it, he must burn in hell for ever."

"To be sure, that is a drawback and no mistake," cried Keawe. "I would not **meddle** with the thing. I can do without a house, thank God; but there is one thing I could not be doing with one **particle,** and that is to be damned."

EXERCISE 1

SELF-TEST: After reading the above selection, do the following. Look at the Master Words below. Underline the words that you think you know. Circle the words that you are less sure about. Draw a square around the words you don't recognize.

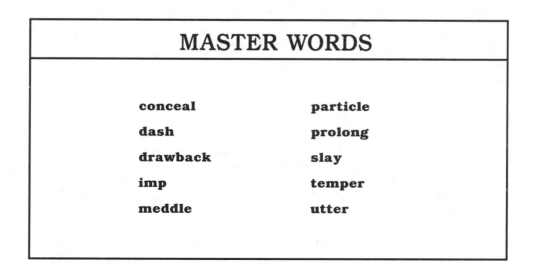

MASTER WORDS

conceal	particle
dash	prolong
drawback	slay
imp	temper
meddle	utter

Read the selection on the preceding page again, this time paying special attention to the ten Master Words. In the (a) spaces provided below, write down what you think is the meaning of the word. After you have attempted a definition for each word, look up the word in a dictionary. In the (b) spaces, copy the appropriate dictionary definition.

1. **conceal** (v.)

    a. _____

    b. _____

2. **dash** (v.)

    a. _____

    b. _____

3. **drawback** (n.)

    a. _____

    b. _____

4. **imp** (n.)

    a. _____

    b. _____

5. **meddle** (v.)

    a. _____

    b. _____

6. **particle** (n.)

    a. _____

    b. _____

7. **prolong** (v.)

    a. _____

    b. _____

8. **slay** (v.)

    a. _____

    b. _____

9. **temper** (v.)

    a. _____

    b. _____

10. **utter** (v.)

    a. _____

    b. _____

Use the following list of synonyms and antonyms to fill in the blanks. Some words have no antonyms. In such cases, the antonym blanks have been marked with an X.

angel	disadvantage	lengthen	pile	shorten	speck
benefit	fling	melt	refrain	spare	stifle
cradle	hide	murder	reveal	speak	toughen
demon	interfere				

	Synonyms	**Antonyms**
1. **dash**	_____	_____
2. **temper**	_____	_____
3. **imp**	_____	_____
4. **utter**	_____	_____
5. **slay**	_____	_____
6. **prolong**	_____	_____
7. **conceal**	_____	_____
8. **drawback**	_____	_____
9. **meddle**	_____	_____
10. **particle**	_____	_____

Decide whether the first pair in the items below are synonyms or antonyms. Then choose the Master Word that shows a similar relation to the word(s) preceding the blank.

1. assured	:undecided	::clump	: _____
2. arena	:stadium	::harden	: _____
3. hesitation	:sureness	::cut	: _____
4. rapid	:unhurried	::ignore	: _____
5. element	:feature	::hurl	: _____
6. certainty	:doubt	::uncover	: _____
7. crouch	:bend down	::evil spirit	: _____
8. parapet	:fence	::kill	: _____
9. perception	:realization	::say	: _____
10. vast	:limited	::good point	: _____

EXERCISE 5

The Master Words in this lesson are repeated below. From the Master Words, choose the appropriate word for the blank in each of the following sentences. Write the word in the numbered space provided at the right.

conceal	drawback	meddle	prolong	temper
dash	imp	particle	slay	utter

1. After he had carefully fashioned the delicate vase, the artist ...?...(d, ed) the glass to make it more durable.

1. _____

2. The story told of (a, an) ...?... who had been imprisoned in a sorcerer's bottle for thousands of years.

2. _____

3. No one could figure out where the magician ...?...(d, ed) the huge playing cards which suddenly appeared on the table.

3. _____

4. With his slingshot the young boy David was able to ...?... the giant Goliath.

4. _____

5. During the heavy downpour, we watched the storm ...?... the rain against the glass.

5. _____

6. When the door opened and closed by itself, Marge was so astonished that she was unable to ...?... a word.

6. _____

7. The only ...?... to the used car was that it was not equipped with an air conditioner.

7. _____

8. We pleaded with Dad to ...?... our camping trip, but he insisted that he had to return to the office.

8. _____

9. Walt claimed that his older sister ...?...(d, ed) in his affairs and read his mail.

9. _____

10. Even (a, an) ...?... of dust on the lens will show up in the finished snapshot.

10. _____

EXERCISE 6

To complete the crossword, choose the Master Word associated with each word or phrase below. Begin each answer in the square having the same number as the clue.

1. to express yourself

2. keep under cover

3. may be done to glass, clay, justice, etc.

4. a molecule or an atom, for instance

5. not a selling point

6. you might wish to do this to your vacation

7. troublemaker

8. mind someone else's business

9. smash to bits

10. what knights do to dragons

Read the following selection to get the general meaning. Read it a second time, paying special attention to the words in dark type. Notice how they are used in sentences. These are Master Words. These are the words you will be working with in this lesson.

Adapted from **Black Beauty**
by Anna Sewell

"Well, sir," John related, "I saw your son whipping, and kicking, and knocking that good little pony about shamefully because he would not leap a gate that was too high for him. The pony behaved well, sir, and showed no **vice**; but at last he just threw up his heels and tipped the young gentleman into the thorn hedge. He wanted me to help him out, but I hope you will excuse me, sir, I did not feel **inclined** to do so. There's no bones broken, sir; he'll only get a few scratches. I love horses, and it **riles** me to see them badly used; it is a bad plan to **aggravate** an animal till he uses his heels; the first time is not always the last."

So we went on, John chuckling all the way home; then he told James about it, who laughed and said, "Served him right. I knew that boy at school; he took great airs on himself because he was a farmer's son; he used to **swagger** about and bully the little boys. I well remember one day, just before afternoon school, I found him at the large window catching flies and pulling off their wings. He did not see me and I gave him a box on the ears that laid him **sprawling** on the floor. Well, angry as I was, I was almost frightened, he roared and **bellowed** in such a style. The boys rushed in from the playground, and the master ran in from the road to see who was being slain. Of course I said fair and square at once what I had done, and why. Then the master talked to all the boys very seriously about cruelty, and said how **hardhearted** and cowardly it was to hurt the weak and the helpless; but what stuck in my mind was this— he said that cruelty was the devil's own **trademark**, and if we saw any one who took pleasure in cruelty we might know who he belonged to, for the devil was a murderer from the beginning, and a **tormentor** to the end."

EXERCISE 1

SELF-TEST: After reading the above selection, do the following. Look at the Master Words below. Underline the words that you think you know. Circle the words that you are less sure about. Draw a square around the words you don't recognize.

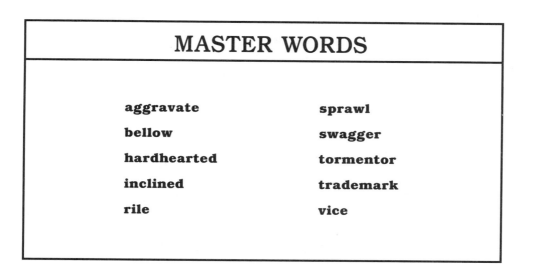

MASTER WORDS

aggravate	sprawl
bellow	swagger
hardhearted	tormentor
inclined	trademark
rile	vice

Read the selection on the preceding page again, this time paying special attention to the ten Master Words. In the (a) spaces provided below, write down what you think is the meaning of the word. After you have attempted a definition for each word, look up the word in a dictionary. In the (b) spaces, copy the appropriate dictionary definition.

1. **aggravate** (v.)

   a. _____

   b. _____

2. **bellow** (v.)

   a. _____

   b. _____

3. **hardhearted** (adj.)

   a. _____

   b. _____

4. **inclined** (adj.)

   a. _____

   b. _____

5. **rile** (v.)

   a. _____

   b. _____

6. **sprawl** (v.)

   a. _____

   b. _____

7. **swagger** (v.)

   a. _____

   b. _____

8. **tormentor** (n.)

   a. _____

   b. _____

9. **trademark** (n.)

   a. _____

   b. _____

10. **vice** (n.)

    a. _____

    b. _____

EXERCISE 3

Use the following list of synonyms and antonyms to fill in the blanks. Some words have no antonyms. In such cases, the antonym blanks have been marked with an X.

anger   irritate   merciless   roar   spread   virtue
bully   kind   protector   shuffle   strut   whisper
calm   likely   reluctant   soothe   trait   wickedness
huddle

	Synonyms	**Antonyms**
1. **vice**		
2. **inclined**		
3. **rile**		
4. **aggravate**		
5. **swagger**		
6. **sprawl**		
7. **bellow**		
8. **hardhearted**		
9. **trademark**		X
10. **tormentor**		

EXERCISE 4

Decide whether the first pair in the items below are synonyms or antonyms. Then choose the Master Word that shows a similar relation to the word(s) preceding the blank.

1. particle :mass ::curl up : _____
2. prolong :decrease ::good habit : _____
3. meddle :let alone ::relieve : _____
4. conceal :expose ::murmur : _____
5. temper :strengthen ::bother : _____
6. drawback :advantage ::caring : _____
7. dash :throw ::prance : _____
8. imp :devil ::torturer : _____
9. slay :murder ::symbol : _____
10. utter :tell ::willing : _____

The Master Words in this lesson are repeated below. From the Master Words, choose the appropriate word for the blank in each of the following sentences. Write the word in the numbered space provided at the right.

aggravate	hardhearted	rile	swagger	trademark
bellow	inclined	sprawl	tormentor	vice

1. The plan to destroy forest land in order to build a recreation area will ...?... many bird-watchers.

1. _____

2. Scott's ...?... smile earned him the nickname of "Grinner."

2. _____

3. Leona spread the newspaper out on the carpet and then ...?...(d, ed) on the floor to read it.

3. _____

4. "What happened to the car?" Mother ...?...(d, ed) when she saw the dented fender.

4. _____

5. Plump Keith admitted sweetly that a love of chocolate was his only ...?... .

5. _____

6. Bicycle riding ...?...(d, ed) an old knee injury he had suffered while playing football.

6. _____

7. Although the actors were talented and the plot was exciting, Tory did not feel ...?... to see the new movie.

7. _____

8. My old ...?..., Chris, finally quit teasing me when I started to ignore his nasty jokes.

8. _____

9. Students thought Mr. Jacobson was extremely ...?... to assign a ten-page paper to be written over vacation.

9. _____

10. Ever since Randy inherited some money from his aunt, he ...?...(s) past his old friends without even a nod.

10. _____

Use at least five Master Words from this lesson to write a scene about one of the following topics. Or create a topic of your own. Write your choice on the blank. Circle the Master Words as you use them.

Possible Topics: Outsmarting the Bully, A Spoiled Day

_____

_____

_____

_____

_____

_____

_____

_____

Read the following selection to get the general meaning. Read it a second time, paying special attention to the words in dark type. Notice how they are used in sentences. These are Master Words. These are the words you will be working with in this lesson.

From **"The Bishop's Candlesticks"**
by Victor Hugo

"Monsieur le Cure," said the man, "you are very good. You take me into your house and light your candles for me. I haven't hid from you what I am, and yet you do not **despise** me."

The bishop touched his hand and said: "This is not my house, it is the house of Christ. It does not ask any comer what he is, but whether he has an **affliction**. You are suffering; you are cold and hungry; be welcome. And do not thank me or tell me that I have taken you into my house; for this is the home of no man, except him who needs a **refuge**. You, who are a traveler, are more at home here than I; whatever is here is yours."

"Stop, Monsieur le Cure," exclaimed the man. "I was cold and hungry when I came in, but you are so kind that now I don't know what I am. All that is gone."

The bishop looked at him again and said, "You have seen much suffering?"

"Yes," said the man. "The ball and chain, the **plank** to sleep on, the heat, the cold, the **lash**, the double chain for nothing, the **dungeon** for a word—even when sick, the chain. The dogs are happier! Nineteen years, and I am forty-six and have a yellow **passport** and that is all."

"Yes," said the bishop, "you have left a place of great suffering. But listen, there will be more joy in heaven over the tears of one **repentant** sinner than over the **salvation** of a hundred good men. If you leave that place with hate and anger against men, you are worthy of **compassion**; if you leave it with good will and gentleness, you are better than any of us."

EXERCISE 1

SELF-TEST: After reading the above selection, do the following. Look at the Master Words below. Underline the words that you think you know. Circle the words that you are less sure about. Draw a square around the words you don't recognize.

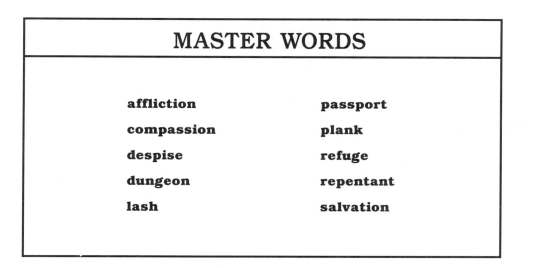

MASTER WORDS

affliction	passport
compassion	plank
despise	refuge
dungeon	repentant
lash	salvation

Read the selection on the preceding page again, this time paying special attention to the ten Master Words. In the (a) spaces provided below, write down what you think is the meaning of the word. After you have attempted a definition for each word, look up the word in a dictionary. In the (b) spaces, copy the appropriate dictionary definition.

1. **affliction** (n.)

    a. _____

    b. _____

2. **compassion** (n.)

    a. _____

    b. _____

3. **despise** (v.)

    a. _____

    b. _____

4. **dungeon** (n.)

    a. _____

    b. _____

5. **lash** (n.)

    a. _____

    b. _____

6. **passport** (n.)

    a. _____

    b. _____

7. **plank** (n.)

    a. _____

    b. _____

8. **refuge** (n.)

    a. _____

    b. _____

9. **repentant** (adj.)

    a. _____

    b. _____

10. **salvation** (n.)

    a. _____

    b. _____

Use the following list of synonyms and antonyms to fill in the blanks. Some words have no antonyms. In such cases, the antonym blanks have been marked with an X.

admire	distress	prison	rescue	sorry
board	document	regretless	scorn	sympathy
cruelty	exposure	relief	shelter	whip
damnation				

	Synonyms	**Antonyms**
1. **despise**	_____	_____
2. **affliction**	_____	_____
3. **refuge**	_____	_____
4. **plank**	_____	X
5. **lash**	_____	X
6. **dungeon**	_____	X
7. **passport**	_____	X
8. **repentant**	_____	_____
9. **salvation**	_____	_____
10. **compassion**	_____	_____

Decide whether the first pair in the items below are synonyms or antonyms. Then choose the Master Word that shows a similar relation to the word(s) preceding the blank.

1. sprawl	:bunch up	::respect	: _____
2. rile	:annoy	::strap	: _____
3. vice	:goodness	::comfort	: _____
4. swagger	:parade	::apologetic	: _____
5. aggravate	:ease	::firing line	: _____
6. bellow	:mumble	::meanness	: _____
7. tormentor	:bully	::dark cell	: _____
8. trademark	:characteristic	::beam	: _____
9. inclined	:eager	::travel permit	: _____
10. hardhearted	:sympathetic	::doom	: _____

The Master Words in this lesson are repeated below. From the Master Words, choose the appropriate word for the blank in each of the following sentences. Write the word in the numbered space provided at the right.

| affliction | despise | lash | plank | repentant |
| compassion | dungeon | passport | refuge | salvation |

1. Before I could take the overseas tour, I had to get (a, an) ...?... . 1._____

2. So great was the student's ...?... for the homeless family that he organized a campaign to help them. 2._____

3. After the prisoner was released, he seemed ...?... about his crimes, and the warden did not expect his return. 3._____

4. Hard-working students ...?... those who cheat to pass a test. 4._____

5. Such ...?...(s) as ringworm and hookworm have been greatly reduced by modern medicines. 5._____

6. The horse's owner said he didn't want his animals beaten and told the jockey not to use the ...?... . 6._____

7. A cabin provided the hunters (a, an) ...?... from the raging blizzard. 7._____

8. Because he had insulted the queen, the court jester was locked for a month in the ...?... . 8._____

9. Gene and Darren carefully stacked the ...?...(s) that would later become the floor of their tree house. 9._____

10. When you are lost—in the woods or on the road—a good compass may be your ...?... . 10._____

Write the Master Word that is associated with each word group below. Then list three things that might be associated with the review word that follows.

1. customs, visa, foreign lands _____

2. prejudice, enemy, crime of hate _____

3. embarrassed, twinge of conscience, make amends _____

4. harbor, monastery, fort _____

5. tragedy, wound, disease _____

6. prisoner, dragons, darkness _____

7. frame, scaffolding, boardwalk _____

8. flog, cat-o'-nine-tails, thong _____

9. setting free, rebirth, redeemer _____

10. Good Samaritan, Mother Teresa, charity _____

Review word: vice (Lesson 2)

_____ _____ _____

Read the following selection to get the general meaning. Read it a second time, paying special attention to the words in dark type. Notice how they are used in sentences. These are Master Words. These are the words you will be working with in this lesson.

Adapted from **The Red Badge of Courage**
by Stephen Crane

One night, as the youth lay in bed, the winds had carried to him the **clangor** of the church bell as some **enthusiast** jerked the rope **frantically** to tell the twisted news of a great battle. This voice of the people rejoicing in the night had made him shiver in a prolonged **ecstasy** of excitement. Later, he had gone down to his mother's room and had spoken thus: "Ma, I'm going to **enlist**."

"Henry, don't you be a fool," his mother had replied. She had then covered her face with the quilt. There was an end to the matter for that night.

Nevertheless, the next morning he had gone to a town that was near his mother's farm and had enlisted in a company that was forming there. When he had returned home his mother was milking the brown cow. Four others stood waiting. "Ma, I've enlisted," he had said to her **diffidently**. There was a short silence. "The Lord's will be done, Henry," she had finally replied, and had then continued to milk the brown cow.

When he had stood in the doorway with his soldier's clothes on his back, and with the light of excitement and expectation in his eyes almost defeating the glow of regret for the home **bonds**, he had seen two tears leaving their trails on his mother's scarred cheeks.

Still, she had disappointed him by saying nothing whatever about returning with his shield or on it. He had privately **primed** himself for a beautiful scene. He had prepared certain sentences which he thought could be used with **touching effect**. But her words destroyed his plans. She had stubbornly peeled potatoes and addressed him as follows: "You watch out, Henry, an' take good care of yerself in this here fighting business—you watch out, an' take good care of yerself. Don't go a-thinkin' you can lick the hull rebel army at the start, because yeh can't. Yer jest one little feller amongst a hull lot of others, and yeh've got to keep quiet an' do what they tell yeh. I know how you are, Henry.

"I've knet yeh eight pair of socks, Henry, and I've put in all yer best shirts, because I want my boy to be jest as warm and comf'able as anybody in the army. Whenever they get holes in 'em, I want yeh to send 'em rightaway back to me, so's I kin dern 'em . . . ."

EXERCISE 1

SELF-TEST: After reading the above selection, do the following. Look at the Master Words below. Underline the words that you think you know. Circle the words that you are less sure about. Draw a square around the words you don't recognize.

MASTER WORDS	
bond	enlist
clangor	enthusiast
diffident	frantic
ecstasy	prime
effect	touching

Read the selection on the preceding page again, this time paying special attention to the ten Master Words. In the (a) spaces provided below, write down what you think is the meaning of the word. After you have attempted a definition for each word, look up the word in a dictionary. In the (b) spaces, copy the appropriate dictionary definition.

1. **bond** (n.)

    a. _____

    b. _____

2. **clangor** (n.)

    a. _____

    b. _____

3. **diffident** (adj.)

    a. _____

    b. _____

4. **ecstasy** (n.)

    a. _____

    b. _____

5. **effect** (n.)

    a. _____

    b. _____

6. **enlist** (v.)

    a. _____

    b. _____

7. **enthusiast** (n.)

    a. _____

    b. _____

8. **frantic** (adj.)

    a. _____

    b. _____

9. **prime** (v.)

    a. _____

    b. _____

10. **touching** (adj.)

    a. _____

    b. _____

Use the following list of synonyms and antonyms to fill in the blanks. Some words have no antonyms. In such cases, the antonym blanks have been marked with an X.

bold   depression   idle   prepare   ringing   tie
calm   dull   moving   quit   silence   timid
cause   enroll   overjoyfulness result   split   wild
critic   fan

	Synonyms	**Antonyms**
1. **clangor**	_____	_____
2. **enthusiast**	_____	_____
3. **frantic**	_____	_____
4. **ecstasy**	_____	_____
5. **enlist**	_____	_____
6. **diffident**	_____	_____
7. **bond**	_____	_____
8. **prime**	_____	_____
9. **touching**	_____	_____
10. **effect**	_____	_____

Decide whether the first pair in the items below are synonyms or antonyms. Then choose the Master Word that shows a similar relation to the word(s) preceding the blank.

1. lash	:whip	::emotional	: _____
2. repentant	:regretful	::gonging	: _____
3. despise	:like	::confident	: _____
4. refuge	:safety	::make ready	: _____
5. affliction	:blessing	::peaceful	: _____
6. compassion	:kindness	::outcome	: _____
7. dungeon	:underground jail	::delight	: _____
8. plank	:timber	::supporter	: _____
9. salvation	:ruin	::separation	: _____
10. passport	:travel papers	::join	: _____

EXERCISE 5

The Master Words in this lesson are repeated below. From the Master Words, choose the appropriate word for the blank in each of the following sentences. Write the word in the numbered space provided at the right.

| bond | diffident | effect | enthusiast | prime |
| clangor | ecstasy | enlist | frantic | touching |

1. The ...?... of the alarm means it is time to begin another day.

1. _____

2. The scrapbook prepared by the students was a sweet, ...?... tribute to the retiring teacher.

2. _____

3. Some health food ...?...(s) refuse to eat anything that isn't naturally grown.

3. _____

4. Although Jean was ...?...(d, ed) for reading her composition, the teacher did not call upon her.

4. _____

5. After three hours of making excuses, shy Rick ...?...(ly) rang his first doorbell as a Christmas card salesperson.

5. _____

6. The ice cream lover was in ...?... over the 31 delicious flavors.

6. _____

7. When Debbie noticed that she had only ten minutes to complete her math test, she became ...?... .

7. _____

8. One ...?... of staying up until the wee hours may be sleepiness the next day.

8. _____

9. The Navy recruiter made sea life appear very attractive, and Glen was persuaded to ...?... .

9. _____

10. A good patch job on a bike tire requires a good ...?... between the patch and the tube.

10. _____

EXERCISE 6

The invented words below are formed from parts of different Master Words from this lesson. Create a definition and indicate the part of speech for each word. The first one is done for you.

ecstafrantic   *(adj.) wildly overjoyed* _____

bondfrantic   _____

clangprime   _____

diffenlist   _____

Now invent your own words by combining parts of the Master Words. Create a definition for each, and indicate the word's part of speech. (You may reuse any of the word parts above in new combinations.)

1. _____   _____

2. _____   _____

Read the following selection to get the general meaning. Read it a second time, paying special attention to the words in dark type. Notice how they are used in sentences. These are Master Words. These are the words you will be working with in this lesson.

Adapted from **"To Build a Fire"**
by Jack London

There was the fire, snapping and **crackling** and promising life with every dancing flame. He started to untie his moccasins. They were coated with ice; the thick German socks were like **sheaths** of iron halfway to the knees; and the moccasin strings were like rods of steel all twisted and knotted as if by fire. For a moment he tugged with his **numb** fingers, then, realizing the **folly** of it, he drew his sheath knife.

But before he could cut the strings, it happened. It was his own fault or, rather, his mistake. He should not have built the fire under the spruce tree. He should have built it in the open. But it had been easier to pull the twigs from the brush and drop them **directly** on the fire. Now the tree under which he had done this carried a weight of snow on its **boughs**. No wind had blown for weeks, and each bough was fully freighted. Each time he had pulled a twig he had given a slight **agitation** to the tree—an agitation scarcely noticeable, so far as he was concerned, but an agitation sufficient to bring about the **disaster**. High up in the tree one bough **capsized** its load of snow. This fell on the boughs beneath, capsizing them. This process continued, spreading out and involving the whole tree. It grew like an **avalanche**, and it descended without warning upon the man and the fire, and the fire was blotted out!

The man was shocked. It was as though he had just heard his own sentence of death. For a moment he sat and stared at the spot where the fire had been. Then he grew very calm. Perhaps the old-timer on Sulphur Creek was right. No man should travel alone in the Klondike after fifty below. If he had only had a trail mate he would have been in no danger now. The trail mate could have built the fire. Well, it was up to him to build the fire over again, and this second time there must be no failure. Even if he succeeded, he would most likely lose some toes. His feet must be badly frozen by now, and there would be some time before the second fire was ready.

—From "To Build a Fire" from Lost Face *by Jack London. Used by permission.*

EXERCISE 1

SELF-TEST: After reading the above selection, do the following. Look at the Master Words below. Underline the words that you think you know. Circle the words that you are less sure about. Draw a square around the words you don't recognize.

MASTER WORDS

agitation	**directly**
avalanche	**disaster**
bough	**folly**
capsize	**numb**
crackle	**sheath**

Read the selection on the preceding page again, this time paying special attention to the ten Master Words. In the (a) spaces provided below, write down what you think is the meaning of the word. After you have attempted a definition for each word, look up the word in a dictionary. In the (b) spaces, copy the appropriate dictionary definition.

1. **agitation** (n.)

    a. _____

    b. _____

2. **avalanche** (n.)

    a. _____

    b. _____

3. **bough** (n.)

    a. _____

    b. _____

4. **capsize** (v.)

    a. _____

    b. _____

5. **crackle** (v.)

    a. _____

    b. _____

6. **directly** (adv.)

    a. _____

    b. _____

7. **disaster** (n.)

    a. _____

    b. _____

8. **folly** (n.)

    a. _____

    b. _____

9. **numb** (adj.)

    a. _____

    b. _____

10. **sheath** (n.)

    a. _____

    b. _____

Use the following list of synonyms and antonyms to fill in the blanks. Some words have no antonyms. In such cases, the antonym blanks have been marked with an X.

balance	deadened	landslide	peace	snap	twig
branch	disturbance	misfortune	roundabout	straight	wisdom
case	foolishness	overturn	sensitive	success	

	Synonyms	**Antonyms**
1. **crackle**	_____	X
2. **sheath**	_____	X
3. **numb**	_____	_____
4. **folly**	_____	_____
5. **directly**	_____	_____
6. **bough**	_____	_____
7. **agitation**	_____	_____
8. **disaster**	_____	_____
9. **capsize**	_____	_____
10. **avalanche**	_____	X

Decide whether the first pair in the items below are synonyms or antonyms. Then choose the Master Word that shows a similar relation to the word(s) preceding the blank.

1. touching	:tender	::unrest	: _____
2. clangor	:ringing	::covering	: _____
3. diffident	:unafraid	::common sense	: _____
4. prime	:undo	::circularly	: _____
5. frantic	:composed	::steady	: _____
6. ecstasy	:happiness	::pop	: _____
7. effect	:reason	::fortune	: _____
8. enthusiast	:booster	::limb	: _____
9. bond	:union	::unfeeling	: _____
10. enlist	:volunteer	::snowslide	: _____

The Master Words in this lesson are repeated below. From the Master Words, choose the appropriate word for the blank in each of the following sentences. Write the word in the numbered space provided at the right.

agitation   bough   crackle   disaster   numb
avalanche   capsize   directly   folly   sheath

1. A sharp stroke of his paddle caused Nate's canoe to ...?... .

1. _____

2. The clumsy hikers, by making the leaves ...?... and the twigs snap, chased away the deer.

2. _____

3. During the severe windstorm, several ...?...(s) were broken from the stately maple trees.

3. _____

4. During the huge ticker tape parade, (a, an) ...?... of confetti was thrown out the windows.

4. _____

5. The hero's entering with an umbrella instead of a rifle was just one of the mistakes that made our school play (a, an) ...?... .

5. _____

6. Before Dr. Wilkinson began stitching, he gave Ted a drug to kill the pain and make his arm ...?... .

6. _____

7. Striking for higher wages caused much ...?... among the workers.

7. _____

8. Kathy's parents insisted that she go ...?... home after the school dance and not stop to eat.

8. _____

9. The frightened man shook as he drew his sword from its ...?... .

9. _____

10. People jeered at the *Clermont,* a steamship built by Robert Fulton in 1807, referring to it as "Fulton's ...?... ."

10. _____

To complete the crossword, choose the Master Word associated with each word or phrase below. Begin each answer in the square having the same number as the clue.

1. skating on thin ice
2. earthquake or hurricane
3. a danger in mountainous areas
4. in a beeline
5. what an overloaded ferry may do
6. covering for a sword
7. moving, shaking, and stirring are examples
8. how your cheek may feel after a dental checkup
9. cereal may do this when you add milk
10. perch for a bird

LESSON 6

Read the following selection to get the general meaning. Read it a second time, paying special attention to the words in dark type. Notice how they are used in sentences. These are Master Words. These are the words you will be working with in this lesson.

From **"The Standard of Living"**
by Dorothy Parker

Always the girls went to walk on Fifth Avenue on their free afternoons, for it was the **ideal** ground for their favorite game. The game could be played anywhere, and indeed, was, but the great shop windows **stimulated** the two players to their best form.

Annabel had invented the game; or rather she had **evolved** it from an old one. Basically, it was no more than the ancient sport of what-would-you-do-if-you-had-a-million-dollars? But Annabel had drawn a new set of rules for it, had narrowed it, pointed it, made it stricter. Like all games, it was the more **absorbing** for being more difficult.

Annabel's **version** went like this: You must suppose that somebody dies and leaves you a million dollars, cool. But there is a condition to the **bequest**. It is stated in the will that you must spend every nickel of the money on yourself.

There lay the **hazard** of the game. If, when playing it, you forgot and listed among your **expenditures** the rental of a new apartment for your family, for example, you lost your turn to the other player. It was **astonishing** how many—and some of them among the experts, too—would **forfeit** all their winnings by such slips.

—Copyright 1941, 1944 by Dorothy Parker. Published in The New Yorker *and* The Portable Dorothy Parker. *(The Viking Press, Inc.)*

EXERCISE 1

SELF-TEST: After reading the above selection, do the following. Look at the Master Words below. Underline the words that you think you know. Circle the words that you are less sure about. Draw a square around the words you don't recognize.

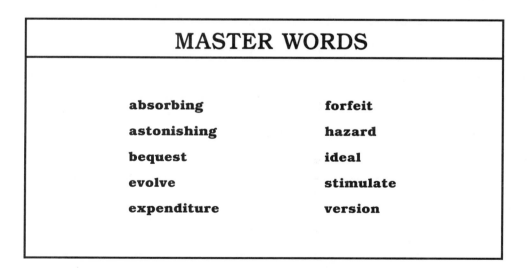

MASTER WORDS

absorbing	forfeit
astonishing	hazard
bequest	ideal
evolve	stimulate
expenditure	version

Read the selection on the preceding page again, this time paying special attention to the ten Master Words. In the (a) spaces provided below, write down what you think is the meaning of the word. After you have attempted a definition for each word, look up the word in a dictionary. In the (b) spaces, copy the appropriate dictionary definition.

1. **absorbing** (adj.)

   a. _____

   b. _____

2. **astonishing** (adj.)

   a. _____

   b. _____

3. **bequest** (n.)

   a. _____

   b. _____

4. **evolve** (v.)

   a. _____

   b. _____

5. **expenditure** (n.)

   a. _____

   b. _____

6. **forfeit** (v.)

   a. _____

   b. _____

7. **hazard** (n.)

   a. _____

   b. _____

8. **ideal** (adj.)

   a. _____

   b. _____

9. **stimulate** (v.)

   a. _____

   b. _____

10. **version** (n.)

   a. _____

   b. _____

Use the following list of synonyms and antonyms to fill in the blanks. Some words have no antonyms. In such cases, the antonym blanks have been marked with an X.

amazing	deaden	excite	form	legacy	payment
block	develop	fascinating	gain	lose	perfect
boring	disinheritance	faulty	income	ordinary	safety
danger					

	Synonyms	**Antonyms**
1. **ideal**	_____	_____
2. **stimulate**	_____	_____
3. **evolve**	_____	_____
4. **absorbing**	_____	_____
5. **version**	_____	X_____
6. **bequest**	_____	_____
7. **hazard**	_____	_____
8. **expenditure**	_____	_____
9. **astonishing**	_____	_____
10. **forfeit**	_____	_____

Decide whether the first pair in the items below are synonyms or antonyms. Then choose the Master Word that shows a similar relation to the word(s) preceding the blank.

1. folly	:good judgment	::defective	: _____
2. agitation	:upheaval	::risk	: _____
3. directly	:crookedly	::profit	: _____
4. capsize	:upend	::give up	: _____
5. sheath	:case	::interesting	: _____
6. crackle	:snap	::gift	: _____
7. disaster	:success	::unexciting	: _____
8. bough	:branch	::arouse	: _____
9. numb	:frozen	::side	: _____
10. avalanche	:slide	::unfold	: _____

EXERCISE 5 ■■■■■■■■■■■■

The Master Words in this lesson are repeated below. From the Master Words, choose the appropriate word for the blank in each of the following sentences. Write the word in the numbered space provided at the right.

absorbing	bequest	expenditure	hazard	stimulate
astonishing	evolve	forfeit	ideal	version

1. In order to save money, one's income must exceed one's ...?...(s).   1. _____

2. Each of the three witnesses had a separate ...?... of the crime.   2. _____

3. Whether man ...?...(d, ed) from lower animals is still a point of argument for many people.   3. _____

4. Although Aunt Ellen's cookbooks did not seem to be a valuable ...?..., they provided hours of enjoyment.   4. _____

5. A crate of peaches that had fallen from a truck onto the highway was (a, an) ...?... to drivers.   5. _____

6. Maria never married because she couldn't match her dreams of the ...?... man to reality.   6. _____

7. Because Barry was an hour late for the wrestling tournament, he had to ...?... his match.   7. _____

8. I exclaimed in surprise when the talented painter revealed the ...?... fact that she was blind.   8. _____

9. So ...?... was Ted's study of Civil War battles that he hated to stop even for dinner.   9. _____

10. The brainstorming session helped ...?... new ideas.   10. _____

EXERCISE 6 ■■■■■■■■■■■■

To complete this puzzle, fill in the Master Word associated with each phrase below. Then unscramble the circled letters to form a Master Word from Lesson 5, and define it.

1. Utopian or perfect   — — — — —

2. hard hats protect against this   Ⓞ — — — — —

3. a good book or movie is this way   Ⓞ — — — — — — — —

4. the watch your grandmother left you in her will   — — — — — Ⓞ —

5. too much of this will make you poor   — — — — — Ⓞ — — —

6. your side of a story   — — Ⓞ — — — —

7. hard to believe   — — — — Ⓞ — — — — —

8. to give up your turn, for example   — — — — — — —

9. caffeine or a thunderclap may do this   — — — — — — — — —

10. to take shape slowly   — — — — — —

Unscrambled word: _____

Definition: _____

Read the following selection to get the general meaning. Read it a second time, paying special attention to the words in dark type. Notice how they are used in sentences. These are Master Words. These are the words you will be working with in this lesson.

Adapted from **"The Adventure of the Speckled Band"** by Arthur Conan Doyle

"Good-morning, madam," said Holmes, cheerily. "My name is Sherlock Holmes. This is my **intimate** friend and **associate**, Dr. Watson, before whom you can speak as freely as before myself. Ha! I am glad to see that Mrs. Hudson has had the good sense to light the fire. Pray draw up to it, and I shall order you a cup of hot coffee, for I observe that you are shivering."

"It is not cold which makes me shiver," said the woman, in a low voice, changing her seat as requested.

"What, then?"

"It is fear, Mr. Holmes. It is terror." She raised her veil as she spoke, and we could see that she was indeed in a **pitiable** state of agitation, her face all drawn and gray, with restless, frightened eyes, like those of some hunted animal. Her features and figure were those of a woman of thirty, but her hair was shot with gray, and her expression was weary and **haggard**. Sherlock Holmes looked at her with one of his quick, all-**comprehensive glances**.

"You must not fear," said he, **soothingly**, bending forward and patting her forearm. "We shall soon set matters right, I have no doubt. You have come in by train this morning, I see."

"You know me, then?"

"No, but I observe the second half of a return ticket in the palm of your left glove. You must have started early, and yet you had a good drive in a dog-cart, along heavy roads, before you reached the station."

The lady gave a violent start, and stared in **bewilderment** at my companion.

"There is no mystery, my dear madam," said he, smiling. "The left arm of your jacket is **spattered** with mud in no less than seven places. The marks are perfectly fresh. There is no **vehicle** save a dog-cart which throws up mud in that way, and then only when you sit on the left-hand side of the driver."

EXERCISE 1

SELF-TEST: After reading the above selection, do the following. Look at the Master Words below. Underline the words that you think you know. Circle the words that you are less sure about. Draw a square around the words you don't recognize.

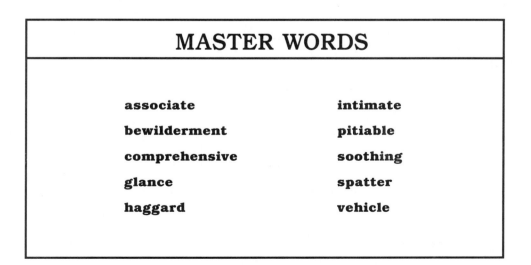

MASTER WORDS

associate	**intimate**
bewilderment	**pitiable**
comprehensive	**soothing**
glance	**spatter**
haggard	**vehicle**

Read the selection on the preceding page again, this time paying special attention to the ten Master Words. In the (a) spaces provided below, write down what you think is the meaning of the word. After you have attempted a definition for each word, look up the word in a dictionary. In the (b) spaces, copy the appropriate dictionary definition.

1. **associate** (n.)

    a. _____

    b. _____

2. **bewilderment** (n.)

    a. _____

    b. _____

3. **comprehensive** (adj.)

    a. _____

    b. _____

4. **glance** (n.)

    a. _____

    b. _____

5. **haggard** (adj.)

    a. _____

    b. _____

6. **intimate** (adj.)

    a. _____

    b. _____

7. **pitiable** (adj.)

    a. _____

    b. _____

8. **soothing** (adj.)

    a. _____

    b. _____

9. **spatter** (v.)

    a. _____

    b. _____

10. **vehicle** (n.)

    a. _____

    b. _____

Use the following list of synonyms and antonyms to fill in the blanks. Some words have no antonyms. In such cases, the antonym blanks have been marked with an X.

aggravating	comforting	distant	limited	peek	stare
car	complete	enviable	partner	rival	understanding
careworn	confusion	fresh	pathetic	splash	wipe
close					

	Synonyms	**Antonyms**
1. **intimate**	_____	_____
2. **associate**	_____	_____
3. **pitiable**	_____	_____
4. **haggard**	_____	_____
5. **comprehensive**	_____	_____
6. **glance**	_____	_____
7. **soothing**	_____	_____
8. **bewilderment**	_____	_____
9. **spatter**	_____	_____
10. **vehicle**	_____	X _____

Decide whether the first pair in the items below are synonyms or antonyms. Then choose the Master Word that shows a similar relation to the word(s) preceding the blank.

1. ideal	:flawed	::withdrawn	:	_____
2. evolve	:disintegrate	::relaxed	:	_____
3. hazard	:threat	::spray	:	_____
4. absorbing	:entertaining	::sad	:	_____
5. bequest	:inheritance	::carriage	:	_____
6. forfeit	:profit	::gaze	:	_____
7. astonishing	:dull	::disturbing	:	_____
8. version	:account	::companion	:	_____
9. expenditure	:expense	::thorough	:	_____
10. stimulate	:motivate	::puzzlement	:	_____

EXERCISE 5

The Master Words in this lesson are repeated below. From the Master Words, choose the appropriate word for the blank in each of the following sentences. Write the word in the numbered space provided at the right.

associate   comprehensive   haggard   pitiable   spatter
bewilderment   glance   intimate   soothing   vehicle

1. (A, An) ...?... in each direction assured Susie that no one would see her leave the surprise gift on Miss Adams' desk.

    1. _____

2. At the beginning of the school year, students were given ...?... health examinations before they could participate in athletics.

    2. _____

3. Many people find ...?... music to be a relaxing end to a busy day.

    3. _____

4. The lunar rover is a unique ...?... especially designed for travel on the moon.

    4. _____

5. Only Shirley's most ...?... friends knew she had once spent time in prison.

    5. _____

6. Mr. Lewis and his business ...?... had rarely disagreed during the twenty years of their partnership.

    6. _____

7. The confusing network of roads at the interchange of four highways left tourists in a state of ...?... .

    7. _____

8. After nursing his sick child all day, Jim looked pale and ...?... .

    8. _____

9. As Todd dropped the chicken leg into the skillet, grease ...?...(d, ed) onto his new white shirt.

    9. _____

10. A sad, ...?... expression on the dog's face would always get him a few table scraps.

    10. _____

EXERCISE 6

Fill in the chart below with the Master Word that fits each set of clues. Part of speech refers to the word's usage in the lesson. Use a dictionary when necessary.

Number of Syllables	Part of Speech	Other Clues	Master Word
4	adjective	a lost child might be this	1. _____
4	noun	a coworker or classmate	2. _____
2	verb	what paint often does	3. _____
3	adjective	like best friends	4. _____
3	noun	train, plane, or auto	5. _____
2	adjective	how you may look after staying up all night	6. _____
4	adjective	a final exam might be this	7. _____
2	adjective	soft music, for instance	8. _____
1	noun	a brief look	9. _____
4	noun	a tough question might cause this	10. _____

LESSON 8

Read the following selection to get the general meaning. Read it a second time, paying special attention to the words in dark type. Notice how they are used in sentences. These are Master Words. These are the words you will be working with in this lesson.

From **Innocents Abroad**
by Mark Twain

Guides know about enough English to **tangle** everything up so that a man can make neither head nor tail of it. They know their story by heart—the history of every statue, painting, cathedral, or other wonder they show you. They know it and tell it as a parrot would—and if you interrupt, and throw them off the track, they have to go back and begin over again. All their lives long, they are employed in showing strange things to foreigners and listening to their bursts of admiration. It is human nature to take delight in exciting admiration. It is what **prompts** children to say "smart" things, and do **absurd** ones, and in other ways "show off" when company is present. It is what makes **gossips** turn out in rain and storms to go and be the first to tell a **startling** bit of news. Think, then, what a **passion** it becomes with a guide, whose privilege it is, every day, to show to strangers wonders that throw them into perfect ecstasies of admiration! He gets so that he could not by any possibility live in a **soberer atmosphere**. After we discovered this, we *never* went into ecstasies any more—we never admired anything—we never showed any but unfeeling faces and stupid **indifference** in the presence of the **sublimest** wonders a guide had to display.

EXERCISE 1

SELF-TEST: After reading the above selection, do the following. Look at the Master Words below. Underline the words that you think you know. Circle the words that you are less sure about. Draw a square around the words you don't recognize.

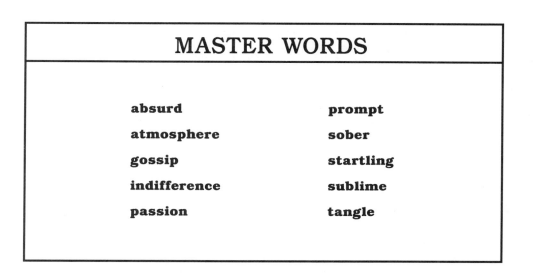

MASTER WORDS

absurd	prompt
atmosphere	sober
gossip	startling
indifference	sublime
passion	tangle

Read the selection on the preceding page again, this time paying special attention to the ten Master Words. In the (a) spaces provided below, write down what you think is the meaning of the word. After you have attempted a definition for each word, look up the word in a dictionary. In the (b) spaces, copy the appropriate dictionary definition.

1. **absurd** (adj.)

    a. _____

    b. _____

2. **atmosphere** (n.)

    a. _____

    b. _____

3. **gossip** (n.)

    a. _____

    b. _____

4. **indifference** (n.)

    a. _____

    b. _____

5. **passion** (n.)

    a. _____

    b. _____

6. **prompt** (v.)

    a. _____

    b. _____

7. **sober** (adj.)

    a. _____

    b. _____

8. **startling** (adj.)

    a. _____

    b. _____

9. **sublime** (adj.)

    a. _____

    b. _____

10. **tangle** (v.)

    a. _____

    b. _____

Use the following list of synonyms and antonyms to fill in the blanks. Some words have no antonyms. In such cases, the antonym blanks have been marked with an X.

coldness	emotion	grand	motivate	serious	surprising
concern	environment	jolly	mute	snarl	talebearer
discourage	expected	lowly	sensible	sort	vacuum
disinterest	foolish				

	Synonyms	**Antonyms**
1. **tangle**	_____	_____
2. **prompt**	_____	_____
3. **absurd**	_____	_____
4. **gossip**	_____	_____
5. **startling**	_____	_____
6. **passion**	_____	_____
7. **sober**	_____	_____
8. **atmosphere**	_____	_____
9. **indifference**	_____	_____
10. **sublime**	_____	_____

Decide whether the first pair in the items below are synonyms or antonyms. Then choose the Master Word that shows a similar relation to the word(s) preceding the blank.

1. intimate	:unfriendly	::organize	: _____
2. haggard	:untroubled	::cheerful	: _____
3. spatter	:slosh	::deep feeling	: _____
4. pitiable	:regrettable	::tattletale	: _____
5. glance	:stare	::unremarkable	: _____
6. soothing	:upsetting	::oppose	: _____
7. vehicle	:carrier	::mood	: _____
8. associate	:companion	::silly	: _____
9. bewilderment	:understanding	::attention	: _____
10. comprehensive	:far-reaching	::splendid	: _____

EXERCISE 5

The Master Words in this lesson are repeated below. From the Master Words, choose the appropriate word for the blank in each of the following sentences. Write the word in the numbered space provided at the right.

absurd	gossip	passion	sober	sublime
atmosphere	indifference	prompt	startling	tangle

1. (A, An) ...?... toward politics caused Mrs. Harrison to view the elections with a lack of enthusiasm.

1. _____

2. The spectacular beauty of the sunset was (a, an) ...?... sight.

2. _____

3. Seventy years ago most people would have said that actually sending a man to the moon was ...?... and ridiculous.

3. _____

4. A neighborhood ...?... may be responsible for the spread of those false rumors.

4. _____

5. Students' complaints about the short lunch period ...?...(d, ed) school officials to lengthen it by fifteen minutes.

5. _____

6. Pete had (a, an) ...?... awakening when both his phone and alarm clock began ringing at once.

6. _____

7. The delicate chain of the necklace was hopelessly ...?...(d, ed).

7. _____

8. In a fit of ...?..., Nick dashed to pieces the battleship he had worked so hard to build.

8. _____

9. Ms. Jonson's use of posters and pictures helped create a relaxed ...?... where students could enjoy learning.

9. _____

10. I saw from Max's ...?... face that he wasn't enjoying the slapstick comedy.

10. _____

EXERCISE 6

Use at least five Master Words from this lesson to write a scene about one of the following topics. Or create a topic of your own. Write your choice on the blank. Circle the Master Words as you use them.

Possible Topics: Lives of the Rich and Famous, Soap Opera at School

_____

_____

_____

_____

_____

_____

_____

_____

Read the following selection to get the general meaning. Read it a second time, paying special attention to the words in dark type. Notice how they are used in sentences. These are Master Words. These are the words you will be working with in this lesson.

Flower City is a **Quonset**-shaped building trimmed in mocha-brown that thinly disguises the shape of the Super-Valu market it once was. On a summer day, when the hot wind puffs across nearby Highway 6, the asphalt parking lot steams and little puddles of blacktop boil up and stick to your shoes.

Inside, Flower City is a plastic jungle—a kind of **botanical** wax museum—where nothing really grows but the Money Tree. The one-time gardener's green thumb is now at the end of the **suburban** housewife's golden arm. And, even if she's short of cash, there's no need to worry, because the big sign on the window urges:

OPEN A FLOWER CITY
REVOLVING CHARGE ACCOUNT.
NO CARRYING CHARGES.
ONE FULL YEAR TO PAY.

As I walked about among Flower City's shabby imitations of nature, I thought back to the many chats I had had with a tiny Japanese woman, who had died three years ago at the age of eighty. Her name was Mrs. Yamamoto, and, as I walked through the aisles lined with "Fade **Resistant**" geraniums and **synthetic** baby's-breath, I thought back to the talk we had the last day I saw her alive.

I remember her moving about against the blue-rimmed, hand-painted china and split bamboo in her living room. She would settle her 4-foot 9-inch figure in the big chair and talk—

her spirit as fine as **porcelain**, her will as tough as teakwood.

"The flowers do not speak, but they understand," she would say, pressing her fingertips together to shape a little steeple of her hands. "Working with life is the great opportunity.

"The arrangement," she said, "must always be in terms of Man and his **relationship** with God and the universe."

Even though a flower had been plucked, for Mrs. Yamamoto it was still flowing with life. "Treat it as healthy; handle it as an infant. It may say nothing, but it feels just the same.

"Our lives are not **enriched** by shabby, breathtaking beauty," she said. "More important is the beauty that expresses family unity, kindness, love, cooperation, and sensitivity."

That is my **recollection** of the last talk I had with Mrs. Yamamoto.

The cash register rang and the clerk, with the letters "Flower City" and "Beulah" stitched in red on her green smock, closed her sale. The woman at the counter picked up her bag filled with lilies of the valley and two "fade resistant" geraniums, but not until she had filled out a coupon and dropped it in the fiberglass barrel.

There would be a drawing next week. The lucky winner would get a styrofoam bird bath and a **sprig** of bittersweet.

—Student

EXERCISE 1

SELF-TEST: After reading the above selection, do the following. Look at the Master Words below. Underline the words that you think you know. Circle the words that you are less sure about. Draw a square around the words you don't recognize.

MASTER WORDS

botanical	relationship
enrich	resistant
porcelain	sprig
Quonset	suburban
recollection	synthetic

Read the selection on the preceding page again, this time paying special attention to the ten Master Words. In the (a) spaces provided below, write down what you think is the meaning of the word. After you have attempted a definition for each word, look up the word in a dictionary. In the (b) spaces, copy the appropriate dictionary definition.

1. **botanical** (adj.)

   a. _____

   b. _____

2. **enrich** (v.)

   a. _____

   b. _____

3. **porcelain** (n.)

   a. _____

   b. _____

4. **Quonset** (n.)

   a. _____

   b. _____

5. **recollection** (n.)

   a. _____

   b. _____

6. **relationship** (n.)

   a. _____

   b. _____

7. **resistant** (adj.)

   a. _____

   b. _____

8. **sprig** (n.)

   a. _____

   b. _____

9. **suburban** (adj.)

   a. _____

   b. _____

10. **synthetic** (adj.)

   a. _____

   b. _____

Use the following list of synonyms and antonyms to fill in the blanks. Some words have no antonyms. In such cases, the antonym blanks have been marked with an X.

amnesia	connection	hut	log	outskirts	tough
artificial	downtown	improve	memory	skyscraper	twig
china	drain	independence	natural	soft	vegetative

	Synonyms	**Antonyms**
1. **Quonset**	_____	_____
2. **botanical**	_____	X _____
3. **suburban**	_____	_____
4. **resistant**	_____	_____
5. **synthetic**	_____	_____
6. **porcelain**	_____	X _____
7. **relationship**	_____	_____
8. **enrich**	_____	_____
9. **recollection**	_____	_____
10. **sprig**	_____	_____

Decide whether the first pair in the items below are synonyms or antonyms. Then choose the Master Word that shows a similar relation to the word(s) preceding the blank.

1. passion	:desire	::ceramic	: _____
2. tangle	:mix up	::recall	: _____
3. sober	:merry	::weak	: _____
4. gossip	:blabbermouth	::shelter	: _____
5. startling	:foreseen	::real	: _____
6. atmosphere	:feeling	::bond	: _____
7. prompt	:discourage	::in-town	: _____
8. absurd	:ridiculous	::cutting	: _____
9. sublime	:supreme	::plantlike	: _____
10. indifference	:interest	::weaken	: _____

EXERCISE 5

The Master Words in this lesson are repeated below. From the Master Words, choose the appropriate word for the blank in each of the following sentences. Write the word in the numbered space provided at the right.

botanical	porcelain	recollection	resistant	suburban
enrich	Quonset	relationship	sprig	synthetic

1. Visitors to the ...?... park will see plants from all around the world.

1. _____

2. (A, An) ...?... of parsley is an attractive decoration for nearly any meat or salad.

2. _____

3. The ...?... fabric was scratchier than real cotton.

3. _____

4. They bought (a, an) ...?... for storage because it was cheap and could be set up quickly.

4. _____

5. When it was dashed against the wall, the delicate ...?... vase shattered into a thousand pieces.

5. _____

6. The cereal makers used special processes to ...?... the grain flakes with vitamins.

6. _____

7. Although "permanent press" fabrics are wrinkle ...?..., they sometimes need a little ironing.

7. _____

8. Matt said he had no ...?... of ever having met Craig and swore they were perfect strangers.

8. _____

9. Overpopulation of cities led to the growth of ...?... areas across the United States.

9. _____

10. After Chris and his father began discussing their differences of opinion, they discovered that their ...?... improved.

10. _____

EXERCISE 6

The invented words below are formed from parts of different Master Words from this lesson. Create a definition and indicate the part of speech for each word. The first one is done for you.

relationspring *(n.) a new and budding relationship* _____

porceltionship _____

botanenrich _____

Quonsistant _____

Now invent your own words by combining parts of the Master Words. Create a definition for each, and indicate the word's part of speech. (You may reuse any of the word parts above in new combinations.)

1. _____ _____

2. _____ _____

Read the following selection to get the general meaning. Read it a second time, paying special attention to the words in dark type. Notice how they are used in sentences. These are Master Words. These are the words you will be working with in this lesson.

From **The Old Man and the Sea**
by Ernest Hemingway

The shark was not an accident. He had come up from deep down in the water as the dark cloud of blood had settled and **dispersed** in the mile deep sea. He had come up so fast and **absolutely** without **caution** that he broke the surface of the blue water and was in the sun. Then he fell back into the sea and picked up the scent and started swimming on the course the **skiff** and the fish had taken.

Sometimes he lost the scent. But he would pick it up again, or have just a trace of it, and he swam fast and hard on the course. He was a very big Mako shark built to swim as fast as the fastest fish in the sea and everything about him was beautiful except his jaws. His back was as blue as a sword fish's and his belly was silver and his hide was smooth and handsome. He was built as a sword fish except for his huge jaws which were tight shut now as he swam fast, just under the surface with his high **dorsal** fin knifing through the water without **wavering**. Inside the closed double lip of his jaws all of his eight rows of teeth were **slanted** inwards. They were not the ordinary pyramid-shaped teeth of most sharks. They were shaped like a man's fingers when they are crisped like claws. They were nearly as long as the fingers of the old man and they had razor-sharp cutting edges on both sides. This was a fish built to feed on all the fishes in the sea that were so fast and strong and well armed that they had no other enemy. Now he speeded up as he smelled the fresher scent and his blue dorsal fin cut the water.

When the old man saw him coming he knew that this was a shark that had no fear at all and would do exactly what he wished. He prepared the harpoon and made the rope **fast** while he watched the shark come on. The rope was short as it lacked what he had cut away to **lash** the fish.

The old man's head was clear and good now and he was full of **resolution** but he had little hope. It was too good to last, he thought. He took one look at the great fish as he watched the shark close in. It might as well have been a dream, he thought. I cannot keep him from hitting me but maybe I can get him. *Dentuso*, he thought. Bad luck to your mother.

—Copyright 1952 by Ernest Hemingway.
Published by Charles Scribner's Sons, New York.

EXERCISE 1

SELF-TEST: After reading the above selection, do the following. Look at the Master Words below. Underline the words that you think you know. Circle the words that you are less sure about. Draw a square around the words you don't recognize.

MASTER WORDS

absolutely	**lash**
caution	**resolution**
disperse	**skiff**
dorsal	**slant**
fast	**waver**

Read the selection on the preceding page again, this time paying special attention to the ten Master Words. In the (a) spaces provided below, write down what you think is the meaning of the word. After you have attempted a definition for each word, look up the word in a dictionary. In the (b) spaces, copy the appropriate dictionary definition.

1. **absolutely** (adv.)

   a. _____

   b. _____

2. **caution** (n.)

   a. _____

   b. _____

3. **disperse** (v.)

   a. _____

   b. _____

4. **dorsal** (adj.)

   a. _____

   b. _____

5. **fast** (adj.)

   a. _____

   b. _____

6. **lash** (v.)

   a. _____

   b. _____

7. **resolution** (n.)

   a. _____

   b. _____

8. **skiff** (n.)

   a. _____

   b. _____

9. **slant** (v.)

   a. _____

   b. _____

10. **waver** (v.)

    a. _____

    b. _____

Use the following list of synonyms and antonyms to fill in the blanks. Some words have no antonyms. In such cases, the antonym blanks have been marked with an X.

back	determination	indecision	rowboat	somewhat	sway
barge	entirely	loose	scatter	stiffen	tilt
bind	front	recklessness	secure	straighten	untie
care	gather				

	Synonyms	**Antonyms**
1. **disperse**	_____	_____
2. **absolutely**	_____	_____
3. **caution**	_____	_____
4. **skiff**	_____	_____
5. **dorsal**	_____	_____
6. **waver**	_____	_____
7. **slant**	_____	_____
8. **fast**	_____	_____
9. **lash**	_____	_____
10. **resolution**	_____	_____

Decide whether the first pair in the items below are synonyms or antonyms. Then choose the Master Word that shows a similar relation to the word(s) preceding the blank.

1. recollection	:forgetfulness	::carelessness	:	_____
2. porcelain	:china	::slope	:	_____
3. Quonset	:shed	::flutter	:	_____
4. resistant	:sturdy	::scatter	:	_____
5. relationship	:association	::rear	:	_____
6. synthetic	:genuine	::untied	:	_____
7. suburban	:urban	::ship	:	_____
8. enrich	:cheapen	::loosen	:	_____
9. sprig	:stem	::decision	:	_____
10. botanical	:vegetative	::completely	:	_____

The Master Words in this lesson are repeated below. From the Master Words, choose the appropriate word for the blank in each of the following sentences. Write the word in the numbered space provided at the right.

absolutely	disperse	fast	resolution	slant
caution	dorsal	lash	skiff	waver

1. Leaders of the American Revolution did not ...?... in their belief that the colonies deserved their independence from England.

1. _____

2. Ken promised his parents that he would use extreme ...?... in riding his new trail bike and follow all the safety rules.

2. _____

3. His strange handwriting tilted to the left instead of ...?...(ing) to the right.

3. _____

4. Sandy ...?...(d, ed) the motorboat to the dock with a rope before helping her grandmother ashore.

4. _____

5. After firemen had put out the fire, the crowd of spectators began to ...?... .

5. _____

6. Melanie swore to the principal that reports she had cheated on the test were ...?... untrue.

6. _____

7. The animal's ...?... quills were no protection when it tumbled onto its back.

7. _____

8. When Mel read the report on smoking and lung cancer, he was filled with new ...?... to "kick the habit."

8. _____

9. Vince's homemade ...?... was the smallest vessel in the Labor Day Parade of Boats.

9. _____

10. Mountain climbers check their gear to see that all ropes are ...?... before the dangerous journey starts.

10. _____

To complete the word spiral, choose the Master Word associated with each phrase below. Start with 1 and fill in each answer clockwise. Be careful! Each new word may overlap the previous word by one or more letters.

1. to sow seeds, for example

2. what a ramp does

3. where you might sit when fishing

4. something tied down firmly is this way

5. completely

6. this might describe the part of the body you sit on

7. do this to attach the sails to the mast

8. yellow traffic lights signal this

9. flags do this in a breeze

10. you might make one on New Year's Day

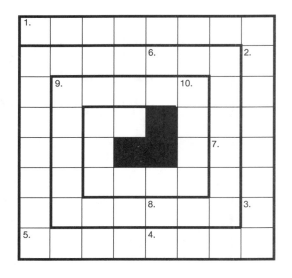

Read the following selection to get the general meaning. Read it a second time, paying special attention to the words in dark type. Notice how they are used in sentences. These are Master Words. These are the words you will be working with in this lesson.

From "The Bottle Imp"
by Robert Louis Stevenson

"I am in for this house," thought he. "Little as I like the way it comes to me, I am in for it now, and I may as well take the good along with the evil."

So he told the **architect** all that he wished, and how he would have that house **furnished**, and about the pictures on the walls and the knickknacks on the tables; and he asked the man plainly for how much he would **undertake** the whole **affair**.

The architect put many questions, and took his pen and made a **computation**; and when he had done he named the very sum that Keawe had **inherited**.

Lopaka and Keawe looked at one another and nodded.

"It is quite clear," thought Keawe, "that I am to have this house, whether or no. It comes from the devil, and I fear I will get little good by that; and of one thing I am sure, I will make no more wishes as long as I have this bottle. But with the house I am **saddled**, and I may as well take the good along with the evil."

So he made his **terms** with the architect, and they signed a paper; and Keawe and Lopaka took ship again and sailed to Australia; for it was **concluded** between them they should not interfere at all, but leave the architect and the bottle imp to build and to **adorn** that house at their own pleasure.

EXERCISE 1

SELF-TEST: After reading the above selection, do the following. Look at the Master Words below. Underline the words that you think you know. Circle the words that you are less sure about. Draw a square around the words you don't recognize.

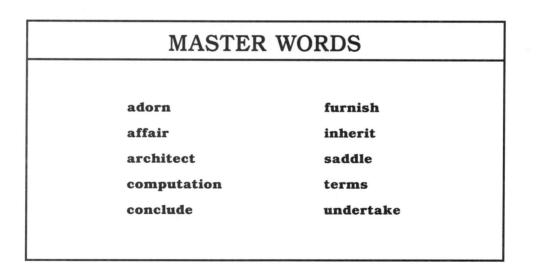

MASTER WORDS

adorn	furnish
affair	inherit
architect	saddle
computation	terms
conclude	undertake

Read the selection on the preceding page again, this time paying special attention to the ten Master Words. In the (a) spaces provided below, write down what you think is the meaning of the word. After you have attempted a definition for each word, look up the word in a dictionary. In the (b) spaces, copy the appropriate dictionary definition.

1. **adorn** (v.)

   a. _____

   b. _____

2. **affair** (n.)

   a. _____

   b. _____

3. **architect** (n.)

   a. _____

   b. _____

4. **computation** (n.)

   a. _____

   b. _____

5. **conclude** (v.)

   a. _____

   b. _____

6. **furnish** (v.)

   a. _____

   b. _____

7. **inherit** (v.)

   a. _____

   b. _____

8. **saddle** (v.)

   a. _____

   b. _____

9. **terms** (n.)

   a. _____

   b. _____

10. **undertake** (v.)

   a. _____

   b. _____

Use the following list of synonyms and antonyms to fill in the blanks. Some words have no antonyms. In such cases, the antonym blanks have been marked with an X.

attempt	business	deface	equip	receive	remove
begin	conditions	designer	figuring	refuse	settle
burden	decorate	donate	guess	relieve	wrecker

	Synonyms	**Antonyms**
1. **architect**	_____	_____
2. **furnish**	_____	_____
3. **undertake**	_____	_____
4. **affair**	_____	X _____
5. **computation**	_____	_____
6. **inherit**	_____	_____
7. **saddle**	_____	_____
8. **terms**	_____	X _____
9. **conclude**	_____	_____
10. **adorn**	_____	_____

Decide whether the first pair in the items below are synonyms or antonyms. Then choose the Master Word that shows a similar relation to the word(s) preceding the blank.

1. slant	:lean	::demands	: _____
2. caution	:watchfulness	::calculation	: _____
3. waver	:flap	::supply	: _____
4. disperse	:assemble	::give	: _____
5. dorsal	:hind	::try	: _____
6. fast	:undone	::start	: _____
7. skiff	:tanker	::blemish	: _____
8. resolution	:purpose	::planner	: _____
9. absolutely	:fully	::activity	: _____
10. lash	:unfasten	::lighten	: _____

The Master Words in this lesson are repeated below. From the Master Words, choose the appropriate word for the blank in each of the following sentences. Write the word in the numbered space provided at the right.

adorn	architect	conclude	inherit	terms
affair	computation	furnish	saddle	undertake

1. Mr. Jefferson warned members of his science club not to ...?... a project that they would be unable to complete.

1. _____

2. Frank Lloyd Wright was (a, an) ...?... noted for suiting his buildings to the natural environment.

2. _____

3. Pioneer children were ...?...(d, ed) with adult responsibilities at an early age.

3. _____

4. The home had been ...?...(d, ed) with lovely chairs and tables from their grandparents' house.

4. _____

5. The United States and the Soviet Union had ...?...(d, ed) several treaties limiting nuclear weapons.

5. _____

6. According to Mom's ...?..., our new car was getting thirty-three miles to the gallon.

6. _____

7. The Watergate ...?... of the 1970s convinced many people that more checks should be placed on the president.

7. _____

8. When Chuck ...?...(d, ed) $20,000, he decided to spend it on a ten-month round-the-world cruise.

8. _____

9. One of the strikers' ...?... for going back to work was higher wages.

9. _____

10. The Williams family ...?...(d, ed) their Christmas tree with old ornaments that had been in the family for years.

10. _____

To complete the crossword, choose the Master Word associated with each word or phrase below. Begin each answer in the square having the same number as the clue.

1. wrap up and call it a day

2. what you might do when a rich relative dies

3. one who works with blueprints

4. a business deal, for example

5. put in tables, chairs, and beds

6. what jewelry does

7. to weigh down

8. you might use a calculator to do this

9. any agreement has them

10. to accept a task

LESSON 12

PART I: From the list below, choose the appropriate word for each sentence that follows. Use each word only once. There will be two words left over.

aggravate	ecstasy	inclined	resistant	utter
comprehensive	enrich	passport	terms	version
computation	forfeit	repentant	trademark	

1. The _____ of an important agreement should be written down.

2. When our team won the game after three overtimes, our fans were in a state of _____.

3. Dad's _____ showed that the regular-size package was a better bargain than the large "economy" size.

4. Frequent visits to the art museum, theater, and library can _____ a person's life.

5. In spite of the cold, rainy weather, Mr. Thompson felt _____ to take his usual walk after dinner.

6. Good looks sometimes serve as (a, an) _____ into the entertainment business.

7. After boasting that he could play "Rhapsody in Blue" on the piano, Randy realized that what he had learned was a simplified _____.

8. By the rules of the game, you must either give up a card or _____ a turn if you can't answer a question.

9. Many doctors suggest that a person have (a, an) _____ medical examination each year.

10. A note using words clipped from a newspaper became the _____ of the mysterious thief.

11. I didn't want to _____ Kent when he was crabby, so I avoided him.

12. The sinner is _____ and will do only good deeds from now on.

PART II: Decide whether the first pair in the items below are synonyms or antonyms. Then choose a Master Word from Lessons 1-11 which shows a similar relation to the word(s) preceding the blank. Do not repeat a Master Word that appears in the first colulmn.

1. frantic   :hysterical   ::tip over   : _____

2. sublime   :majestic   ::difficulty   : _____

3. conceal   :disguise   ::enthusiasm   : _____

4. recollection   :absentmindedness   ::reasonable   : _____

5. compassion   :heartlessness   ::damnation   : _____

PART III: From the list below, choose the appropriate word for each sentence that follows. Use each word only once. There will be two words left over.

affliction	disperse	indifference	sprawl	synthetic
agitation	expenditure	intimate	stimulate	waver
disaster	gossip	prolong	suburban	

1. Mick hates long meetings and won't _____ a discussion a moment longer than necessary.

2. By overcoming her _____(s) of blindness and deafness, Helen Keller inspired thousands of people.

3. Building a model of Shakespeare's Globe Theatre required a great _____ of time.

4. Because of television and satellites, news can be _____(d, ed) throughout the world in a matter of minutes.

5. Nylon is (a, an) _____ fabric made by humans from coal, air, and water.

6. Generally, houses in _____ areas were built more recently than those in inner cities.

7. Whenever Cal's parents would see him _____(d, ed) on the furniture, they would tell him to sit up like a gentleman.

8. The local _____ spread the news around town like wildfire.

9. I knew a storm was approaching when I saw the _____ of the wind-swept trees.

10. Secretary Halson had _____ knowledge of the president's life but carefully guarded these private details.

11. The fascinating movie on King Tut's tomb helped _____ curiosity about ancient Egypt.

12. I am tired of Pat's _____ to politics; she never seems to care who is running the mayor's office, the Senate, or even the White House.

PART IV: Decide whether the first pair in the items below are synonyms or antonyms. Then choose a Master Word from Lessons 1-11 which shows a similar relation to the word(s) preceding the blank. Do not repeat a Master Word that appears in the first column.

1. numb   :responsive   ::praise   : _____

2. bewilderment :muddle   ::best   : _____

3. caution   :foolhardiness   ::bold   : _____

4. furnish   :supply   ::tackle   : _____

5. resolution   :uncertainty   ::profit   : _____

LESSON 13

Read the following selection to get the general meaning. Read it a second time, paying special attention to the words in dark type. Notice how they are used in sentences. These are Master Words. These are the words you will be working with in this lesson.

From **The Red Badge of Courage**
by Stephen Crane

The two infantrymen could hear nothing until finally [the general] asked: "What **troops** can you spare?"

The officer who rode like a cowboy **reflected** for an instant. "Well," he said, "I had to order in th' 12th to help th' 76th, an' I haven't really got any. But there's th' 304th. They fight like a lot 'a mule drivers. I can spare them best of any."

The youth and his friend **exchanged** glances of **astonishment**.

The general spoke sharply. "Get 'em ready, then. I'll watch **developments** from here, an' send you word when t' start them. It'll happen in five minutes."

As the other officer tossed his fingers toward his cap and wheeling his horse, started away, the general called out to him in a sober voice:

"I don't believe many of your mule drivers will get back."

The other shouted something in reply. He smiled.

With scared faces, the youth and his companion hurried back to the line.

These happenings had occupied an **incredibly** short time, yet the youth felt that in them he had been made aged. New eyes were given to him. And the most startling thing was to learn suddenly that he was very **insignificant**. The officer spoke of the **regiment** as if he **referred** to a broom. Some part of the woods needed sweeping, perhaps, and he **merely** indicated a broom in a tone properly indifferent to its fate. It was war, no doubt, but it appeared strange.

EXERCISE 1

SELF-TEST: After reading the above selection, do the following. Look at the Master Words below. Underline the words that you think you know. Circle the words that you are less sure about. Draw a square around the words you don't recognize.

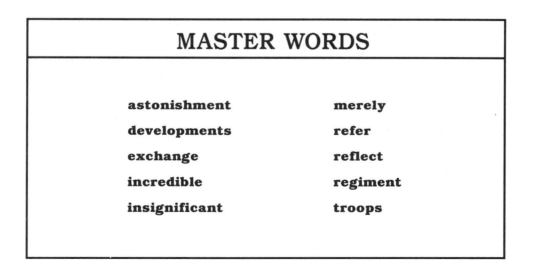

MASTER WORDS

astonishment	merely
developments	refer
exchange	reflect
incredible	regiment
insignificant	troops

Read the selection on the preceding page again, this time paying special attention to the ten Master Words. In the (a) spaces provided below, write down what you think is the meaning of the word. After you have attempted a definition for each word, look up the word in a dictionary. In the (b) spaces, copy the appropriate dictionary definition.

1. **astonishment** (n.)

    a. _____

    b. _____

2. **developments** (n.)

    a. _____

    b. _____

3. **exchange** (v.)

    a. _____

    b. _____

4. **incredible** (adj.)

    a. _____

    b. _____

5. **insignificant** (adj.)

    a. _____

    b. _____

6. **merely** (adv.)

    a. _____

    b. _____

7. **refer** (v.)

    a. _____

    b. _____

8. **reflect** (v.)

    a. _____

    b. _____

9. **regiment** (n.)

    a. _____

    b. _____

10. **troops** (n.)

    a. _____

    b. _____

Use the following list of synonyms and antonyms to fill in the blanks. Some words have no antonyms. In such cases, the antonym blanks have been marked with an X.

amazement	civilians	ignore	mention	simply	trade
believable	consider	important	minor	soldiers	unbelievable
changes	hoard	indifference	regression	suppress	unit

	Synonyms	**Antonyms**
1. **troops**	_____	_____
2. **reflect**	_____	_____
3. **exchange**	_____	_____
4. **astonishment**	_____	_____
5. **developments**	_____	_____
6. **incredible**	_____	_____
7. **insignificant**	_____	_____
8. **regiment**	_____	X
9. **refer**	_____	_____
10. **merely**	_____	X

Decide whether the first pair in the items below are synonyms or antonyms. Then choose the Master Word that shows a similar relation to the word(s) preceding the blank.

1. terms	:conditions	::only	: _____
2. computation	:prediction	::imaginable	: _____
3. inherit	:will	::overlook	: _____
4. furnish	:provide	::military	: _____
5. conclude	:open	::keep	: _____
6. adorn	:deface	::noticeable	: _____
7. undertake	:tackle	::wonder	: _____
8. saddle	:free	::unconcern	: _____
9. architect	:designer	::squad	: _____
10. affair	:business	::progress	: _____

The Master Words in this lesson are repeated below. From the Master Words, choose the appropriate word for the blank in each of the following sentences. Write the word in the numbered space provided at the right.

astonishment   exchange   insignificant   refer   regiment
developments   incredible   merely   reflect   troops

1. The amount of annual rainfall in desert areas is ...?... .

1. _____

2. Several magazines were eager to run the ...?... story of the couple's forty-day struggle for survival in the Yukon.

2. _____

3. Bob Hope often spent part of the Christmas season entertaining American ...?... overseas.

3. _____

4. Ann assured Duane that her mother was not being nosy but was ...?... trying to make conversation.

4. _____

5. The detective promised to keep us informed of ...?... in the case of our stolen property.

5. _____

6. The crowd rose to their feet in ...?... when the pole vaulter broke the world record by a foot.

6. _____

7. Because the dress she received for her birthday was too small, Maggie ...?...(d, ed) it for a larger one.

7. _____

8. The sergeant put the ...?... through tough drills, testing the soldiers' ability to understand commands.

8. _____

9. Whenever the opportunity arose, the history teacher would ...?... to his own combat experience.

9. _____

10. Spending a few moments each evening ...?...(ing) on the day's events can be a worthwhile habit.

10. _____

To complete the word spiral, choose the Master Word associated with each phrase below. Start with 1 and fill in each answer clockwise. Be careful! Each new word may overlap the previous word by one or more letters.

1. force commanded by officer of high rank

2. a lottery winner might be filled with this

3. a flying elephant, for example

4. we often do this with gifts

5. point out or mention

6. thoughtful people, as well as mirrors, do this

7. "nothing more than"

8. events as they unfold

9. a speck of dust, for example

10. also called "warriors" and "leathernecks"

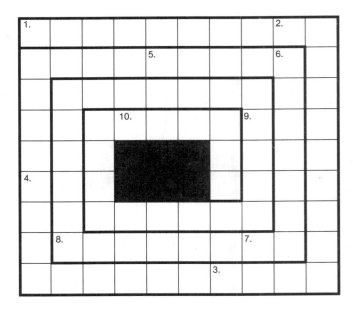

LESSON 14

Read the following selection to get the general meaning. Read it a second time, paying special attention to the words in dark type. Notice how they are used in sentences. These are Master Words. These are the words you will be working with in this lesson.

Adapted from **Robinson Crusoe**
by Daniel Defoe

All my life I had desired nothing save but to go to sea. Both my father and my mother thought ill of such a plan and set about to fit me for the law. Being one day at Hull, having no idea of leaving home immediately, I chanced upon a companion who was about to sail to London in his father's ship. With that bait common to seafaring men, namely that my passage should cost me nothing, he prompted me to go with them. I sought **counsel** of neither my father nor my mother any more, nor so much as sent them word of my leaving. Without asking God's blessing or my father's, and without a thought to the future, on the first of September, 1651, I went on board a ship bound for London.

Never any young adventurer's **misfortunes**, I believe, began sooner or continued longer than mine. The ship was no sooner gotten out of the Humber, but the wind began to blow, and the waves to rise in a most frightful manner; and as I had never been at sea before, I was most **inexpressibly** sick in body, and terrified in mind. I began now seriously to reflect upon what I had done, and how **justly** I was **overtaken** by the judgment of Heaven for my **wickedness** in leaving my father's house, and abandoning my duty; all the good counsel of my parents, my father's tears and my mother's **entreaties**, came now fresh into my mind, and my conscience, which was not yet come to the pitch of hardness to which it has been since, **reproached** me with the **contempt** of advice, and the **breach** of my duty to God and my father.

EXERCISE 1

SELF-TEST: After reading the above selection, do the following. Look at the Master Words below. Underline the words that you think you know. Circle the words that you are less sure about. Draw a square around the words you don't recognize.

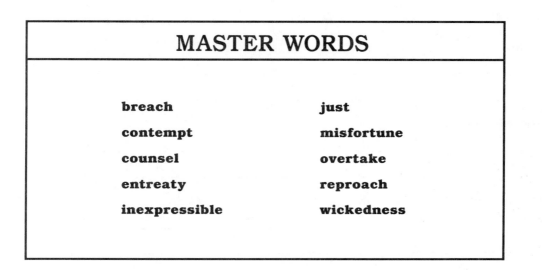

MASTER WORDS	
breach	just
contempt	misfortune
counsel	overtake
entreaty	reproach
inexpressible	wickedness

Read the selection on the preceding page again, this time paying special attention to the ten Master Words. In the (a) spaces provided below, write down what you think is the meaning of the word. After you have attempted a definition for each word, look up the word in a dictionary. In the (b) spaces, copy the appropriate dictionary definition.

1. **breach** (n.)

   a. _____

   b. _____

2. **contempt** (n.)

   a. _____

   b. _____

3. **counsel** (n.)

   a. _____

   b. _____

4. **entreaty** (n.)

   a. _____

   b. _____

5. **inexpressible** (adj.)

   a. _____

   b. _____

6. **just** (adj.)

   a. _____

   b. _____

7. **misfortune** (n.)

   a. _____

   b. _____

8. **overtake** (v.)

   a. _____

   b. _____

9. **reproach** (v.)

   a. _____

   b. _____

10. **wickedness** (n.)

    a. _____

    b. _____

Use the following list of synonyms and antonyms to fill in the blanks. Some words have no antonyms. In such cases, the antonym blanks have been marked with an X.

advice	describable	misguidance	plea	scorn	unfair
catch	evil	obedience	praise	trail	untellable
criticize	goodness	objective	respect	trouble	violation
denial	luck				

	Synonyms	**Antonyms**
1. **counsel**	_____	_____
2. **misfortune**	_____	_____
3. **inexpressible**	_____	_____
4. **just**	_____	_____
5. **overtake**	_____	_____
6. **wickedness**	_____	_____
7. **entreaty**	_____	_____
8. **reproach**	_____	_____
9. **contempt**	_____	_____
10. **breach**	_____	_____

EXERCISE 4 ▰▰▰

Decide whether the first pair in the items below are synonyms or antonyms. Then choose the Master Word that shows a similar relation to the word(s) preceding the blank.

1. merely	:simply	::guidance	:	_____
2. troops	:citizens	::definable	:	_____
3. incredible	:ordinary	::approval	:	_____
4. reflect	:study	::request	:	_____
5. regiment	:outfit	::reach	:	_____
6. refer	:omit	::decency	:	_____
7. exchange	:withhold	::one-sided	:	_____
8. insignificant	:slight	::tragedy	:	_____
9. astonishment	:boredom	::loyalty	:	_____
10. developments	:advancements	::scold	:	_____

The Master Words in this lesson are repeated below. From the Master Words, choose the appropriate word for the blank in each of the following sentences. Write the word in the numbered space provided at the right.

| breach | counsel | inexpressible | misfortune | reproach |
| contempt | entreaty | just | overtake | wickedness |

1. Bret ignored his mother's ...?... not to enlist in the army, though she pleaded for hours.

1. _____

2. The manager ...?...(d, ed) Marilyn for reporting to work an hour late.

2. _____

3. Just a few yards from the finish line, Ben prepared to ...?... the leading runner in the race.

3. _____

4. Dad scorned able-bodied people who refused to look for work, and he could not hide his ...?... .

4. _____

5. Before deciding which courses to take, Judy sought the ...?... of her teachers and her parents.

5. _____

6. The death of his parents was the greatest ...?... in Ivan's life.

6. _____

7. After Simon had broken several terms of the agreement, he was sued for ...?... of contract.

7. _____

8. Cutting off a person's hand for stealing a loaf of bread does not seem (a, an) ...?... punishment to most Americans.

8. _____

9. The ...?... of the villain makes the hero seem even more admirable.

9. _____

10. The immigrants' joy in reaching a land of freedom was ...?... .

10. _____

Order the words in each item from *least* to *most.* Use the abbreviations *L* for "least" and *M* for "most." Leave the line before the word of the middle degree blank. The first word provides a clue about how to arrange the words. See the example.

digging: __M__excavate __L__scratch ____furrow
(*Scratch* indicates the least digging; *excavate* indicates the most digging.)

1. misbehavior: ____playfulness ____wickedness ____disobedience
2. tragic: ____misfortune ____slip-up ____disaster
3. criticism: ____reproach ____condemn ____frown upon
4. dishonesty: ____betrayal ____breach ____white lie
5. approval: ____displeasure ____favor ____contempt
6. insistent: ____demand ____suggestion ____entreaty
7. explainable: ____inexpressible ____unthinkable ____describable
8. guidance: ____inform ____command ____counsel
9. progress: ____surpass ____trail ____overtake
10. fair: ____just ____open-minded ____biased

LESSON 15

Read the following selection to get the general meaning. Read it a second time, paying special attention to the words in dark type. Notice how they are used in sentences. These are Master Words. These are the words you will be working with in this lesson.

From "The Adventure of the Speckled Band" by Arthur Conan Doyle

"I knew that we should find a **ventilator** before ever we came to Stoke Moran."

"My dear Holmes!"

"Oh, yes, I did. You remember in her **statement** she said that her sister could smell Dr. Roylott's cigar. Now, of course that suggested at once that there must be a communication between the two rooms. It could only be a small one, or it would have been remarked upon at the coroner's **inquiry**. I **deduced** a ventilator."

"But what harm can there be in that?"

"Well, there is at least a curious **coincidence** of dates. A ventilator is made, a cord is hung, and a lady who sleeps in the bed dies. Does not that strike you?"

"I cannot as yet see any connection."

"Did you observe anything very **peculiar** about that bed?"

"No."

"It was **clamped** to the floor. Did you ever see a bed fastened like that before?"

"I cannot say that I have."

"The lady could not move her bed. It must always be in the same **relative** position to the ventilator and to the rope—for so we may call it, since it was clearly never meant for a bell-pull."

"Holmes," I cried, "I seem to see dimly what you are hinting at. We are only just in time to prevent some **subtle** and horrible crime."

"Subtle enough and horrible enough. When a doctor does go wrong, he is the first of criminals. He has **nerve** and he has knowledge. Palmer and Pritchard were among the heads of their profession. This man strikes even deeper, but I think, Watson, that we shall be able to strike deeper still. But we shall have horrors enough before the night is over; for goodness' sake let us have a quiet pipe, and turn our minds for a few hours to something more cheerful."

EXERCISE 1

SELF-TEST: After reading the above selection, do the following. Look at the Master Words below. Underline the words that you think you know. Circle the words that you are less sure about. Draw a square around the words you don't recognize.

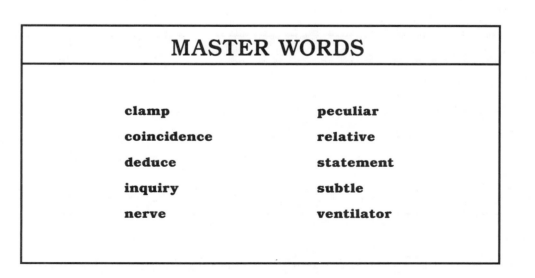

MASTER WORDS

clamp	peculiar
coincidence	relative
deduce	statement
inquiry	subtle
nerve	ventilator

Read the selection on the preceding page again, this time paying special attention to the ten Master Words. In the (a) spaces provided below, write down what you think is the meaning of the word. After you have attempted a definition for each word, look up the word in a dictionary. In the (b) spaces, copy the appropriate dictionary definition.

1. **clamp** (v.)

   a. _____

   b. _____

2. **coincidence** (n.)

   a. _____

   b. _____

3. **deduce** (v.)

   a. _____

   b. _____

4. **inquiry** (n.)

   a. _____

   b. _____

5. **nerve** (n.)

   a. _____

   b. _____

6. **peculiar** (adj.)

   a. _____

   b. _____

7. **relative** (adj.)

   a. _____

   b. _____

8. **statement** (n.)

   a. _____

   b. _____

9. **subtle** (adj.)

   a. _____

   b. _____

10. **ventilator** (n.)

    a. _____

    b. _____

Use the following list of synonyms and antonyms to fill in the blanks. Some words have no antonyms. In such cases, the antonym blanks have been marked with an X.

absolute	comparative	design	glaring	investigation	release
account	courage	elusive	grip	ordinary	unusual
chance	cowardice	fan	guess	reason	

	Synonyms	**Antonyms**
1. **ventilator**	_____	X _____
2. **statement**	_____	X _____
3. **coincidence**	_____	_____
4. **inquiry**	_____	X _____
5. **deduce**	_____	_____
6. **peculiar**	_____	_____
7. **clamp**	_____	_____
8. **relative**	_____	_____
9. **subtle**	_____	_____
10. **nerve**	_____	_____

Decide whether the first pair in the items below are synonyms or antonyms. Then choose the Master Word that shows a similar relation to the word(s) preceding the blank.

1. contempt	:admiration	::usual	: _____
2. counsel	:direction	::accident	: _____
3. inexpressible	:indescribable	::examination	: _____
4. wickedness	:uprightness	::independent	: _____
5. entreaty	:appeal	::conclude	: _____
6. overtake	:catch	::declaration	: _____
7. just	:prejudiced	::fearfulness	: _____
8. misfortune	:good luck	::noticeable	: _____
9. reproach	:criticize	::blower	: _____
10. breach	:faithfulness	::loosen	: _____

The Master Words in this lesson are repeated below. From the Master Words, choose the appropriate word for the blank in each of the following sentences. Write the word in the numbered space provided at the right.

clamp	deduce	nerve	relative	subtle
coincidence	inquiry	peculiar	statement	ventilator

1. Dale ...?...(d, ed) the new headlight onto his bike in preparation for the 100-mile bike-a-thon.

1. _____

2. Congress began (a, an) ...?... into its members' expense accounts.

2. _____

3. From the clues, the detective ...?...(d, ed) that the murderer was a left-handed person no taller than 5 feet 8 inches.

3. _____

4. Poised on the high diving board, Tammy suddenly lost her ...?... and used the ladder to climb down.

4. _____

5. Although in her original ...?... the witness had described the suspect, later she could not identify the man.

5. _____

6. The platypus, with its strange body—and feet and bill like a duck— is one of the most ...?... animals on the face of the earth.

6. _____

7. The ...?... value of U.S. dollars depends on economic factors around the world.

7. _____

8. It was (a, an) ...?... that Mary's tire went flat right in front of a service station.

8. _____

9. When the ...?... ceased working, the air quickly became stuffy.

9. _____

10. The ...?... plot involving agents and double agents made the identity of the master spy difficult to guess.

10. _____

Fill in the chart below with the Master Word that fits each set of clues. Part of speech refers to the word's usage in the lesson. Use a dictionary when necessary.

Number of Syllables	Part of Speech	Other Clues	Master Word
3	noun	an attempt to find out facts	1. _____
1	verb	hold fast	2. _____
1	noun	it takes this to face a problem	3. _____
2	noun	your story about an incident	4. _____
3	adjective	humidity, as well as some pronouns and people, can be this	5. _____
2	adjective	loud colors are not this	6. _____
2	verb	to judge on the basis of clues	7. _____
4	noun	use this to clear a musty room	8. _____
3	adjective	like a three-dollar bill	9. _____
4	noun	chance meeting of long-lost friends	10. _____

Read the following selection to get the general meaning. Read it a second time, paying special attention to the words in dark type. Notice how they are used in sentences. These are Master Words. These are the words you will be working with in this lesson.

From "The Lesson of the Birds"
a Pawnee tale

One day a man whose mind was **receptive** to the teaching of the powers wandered on the prairie. As he walked, his eyes upon the ground, he **spied** a bird's nest hidden in the grass, and **arrested** his feet just in time to prevent stepping on it. He paused to look at the little nest tucked away so **snug** and warm, and noted that it held six eggs and that a peeping sound came from some of them. While he watched, one moved and soon a tiny bill pushed through the shell, uttering a **shrill** cry. At once the parent birds answered and he looked up to see where they were. They were not far off; they were flying about in search of food, chirping the while to each other and now and then calling to the little one in the nest.

The **homely** scene stirred the heart and the thoughts of the man as he stood there under the clear sky, glancing upward toward the old birds and then down to the helpless young in the nest at his feet. As he looked he thought of his people, who were so often careless and thoughtless of their children's needs, and his mind **brooded** over the matter. After many days he desired to see the nest again. So he went to the place where he had found it, and there it was as safe as when he left it. But a change had taken place. It was now full to overflowing with little birds, who were stretching their wings, balancing on their little legs and making ready to fly, while the parents with encouraging calls were **coaxing** the **fledglings** to venture forth.

"Ah!" said the man, "if my people would only learn of the birds, and, like them, care for their young and provide for their future, homes would be full and happy, and our tribe be strong and **prosperous**."

When this man became a priest, he told the story of the bird's nest and sang its song; and so it has come down to us from the days of our fathers.

EXERCISE 1

SELF-TEST: After reading the above selection, do the following. Look at the Master Words below. Underline the words that you think you know. Circle the words that you are less sure about. Draw a square around the words you don't recognize.

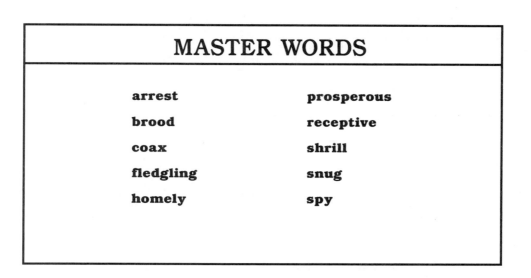

MASTER WORDS

arrest	prosperous
brood	receptive
coax	shrill
fledgling	snug
homely	spy

Read the selection on the preceding page again, this time paying special attention to the ten Master Words. In the (a) spaces provided below, write down what you think is the meaning of the word. After you have attempted a definition for each word, look up the word in a dictionary. In the (b) spaces, copy the appropriate dictionary definition.

1. **arrest** (v.)

    a. _____

    b. _____

2. **brood** (v.)

    a. _____

    b. _____

3. **coax** (v.)

    a. _____

    b. _____

4. **fledgling** (n.)

    a. _____

    b. _____

5. **homely** (adj.)

    a. _____

    b. _____

6. **prosperous** (adj.)

    a. _____

    b. _____

7. **receptive** (adj.)

    a. _____

    b. _____

8. **shrill** (adj.)

    a. _____

    b. _____

9. **snug** (adj.)

    a. _____

    b. _____

10. **spy** (v.)

    a. _____

    b. _____

Use the following list of synonyms and antonyms to fill in the blanks. Some words have no antonyms. In such cases, the antonym blanks have been marked with an X.

accepting	cozy	low-pitched	poor	stately	uncomfortable
adult	discourage	miss	simple	stop	urge
baby	disregard	notice	start	successful	worry
close-minded	high-pitched				

	Synonyms	**Antonyms**
1. **receptive**	_____	_____
2. **spy**	_____	_____
3. **arrest**	_____	_____
4. **snug**	_____	_____
5. **shrill**	_____	_____
6. **homely**	_____	_____
7. **brood**	_____	_____
8. **coax**	_____	_____
9. **fledgling**	_____	_____
10. **prosperous**	_____	_____

Decide whether the first pair in the items below are synonyms or antonyms. Then choose the Master Word that shows a similar relation to the word(s) preceding the blank.

1. peculiar	:typical	::unlivable	:	_____
2. coincidence	:luck	::growing	:	_____
3. inquiry	:research	::catch sight of	:	_____
4. relative	:unrelated	::grand	:	_____
5. deduce	:figure out	::consider	:	_____
6. statement	:report	::open-minded	:	_____
7. nerve	:daring	::encourage	:	_____
8. subtle	:obvious	::grown-up	:	_____
9. clamp	:unfasten	::deep-sounding	:	_____
10. ventilator	:air conditioner	::halt	:	_____

The Master Words in this lesson are repeated below. From the Master Words, choose the appropriate word for the blank in each of the following sentences. Write the word in the numbered space provided at the right.

arrest	coax	homely	receptive	snug
brood	fledgling	prosperous	shrill	spy

1. On cold winter evenings Grandma was ...?... and warm in her favorite chair by the fireplace.

1. _____

2. At least for the moment, the spread of the disease had been ...?...(d, ed), thanks to the new medicine.

2. _____

3. Even in (a, an) ...?... nation like the United States are people who lack the necessities of life.

3. _____

4. "I ...?... land!" the sailor cried from the crow's nest of the old Yankee clipper ship.

4. _____

5. The committee responsible for planning the class party was warmly ...?... to suggestions from other members of the class.

5. _____

6. The ...?... was soon out of the nest, exploring the tree.

6. _____

7. The more Max ...?...(d, ed) over the argument with his sister, the worse he felt about losing control of his temper.

7. _____

8. After being ...?...(d, ed) for an hour, Tweety, the canary, finally returned to his cage.

8. _____

9. Karen's whistle was so ...?... that I heard it over the sirens.

9. _____

10. The cooking utensils hanging on the wall gave the kitchen (a, an) ...?... appearance.

10. _____

Write the Master Word that is associated with each word group below. Then list three things that might be associated with the review word that follows.

1. satellite dish, ears, suggestion box _____

2. bed, cottage, girdle _____

3. sweet-talk, win over, butter up _____

4. whistle, smoke detector, scream _____

5. log cabin, plain clothes, down-home cooking _____

6. fawn, youth, newcomer _____

7. roadblock, heart attack, detention _____

8. clue, misspelling, piece of lint _____

9. long silences, nail-biting, frown _____

10. mansion, well-being, Rolls-Royce _____

Review word: nerve (Lesson 15)

_____ _____ _____

Read the following selection to get the general meaning. Read it a second time, paying special attention to the words in dark type. Notice how they are used in sentences. These are Master Words. These are the words you will be working with in this lesson.

Adapted from **Around the World in Eighty Days** by Jules Verne

The first few days of the voyage passed prosperously, amid favorable weather and **propitious** winds, and they soon came in sight of the great Andaman, the principal of the islands in the Bay of Bengal, with its **picturesque** Saddle Peak, two thousand four hundred feet high, **looming** above the waters. The steamer passed along near the shores, but the savage Papuans, who are in the lowest scale of humanity, but are not, as has been **asserted**, cannibals, did not make their appearance.

The **panorama** of the islands, as they steamed by them, was **superb**. Vast forests of palms, arecs, bamboo, teakwood, of the gigantic mimosa, and tree-like ferns covered the foreground, while behind, the graceful outlines of the mountains were traced against the sky; and along the coasts **swarmed** thousands of precious swallows. The varied landscape **afforded** by the Andaman Islands was soon passed, however, and the "Rangoon" rapidly approached the Straits of Malacca, which give **access** to the China seas.

What was Detective Fix, so unluckily drawn on from country to country, doing all this while? He had managed to board the "Rangoon" at Calcutta without being seen by Passepartout, after leaving orders that, if the **warrant** should arrive, it should be forwarded to him at Hong Kong; and he hoped to conceal his presence to the end of the voyage. It would have been difficult to explain why he was on board without awaking Passepartout's suspicions, who thought him still at Bombay.

All the detective's hopes and wishes were now centered on Hong Kong; for the steamer's stay at Singapore would be too brief to allow him to take any steps there. The arrest must be made at Hong Kong, or the robber would probably escape him for ever. Hong Kong was the last English ground on which he would set foot; beyond, China, Japan, America offered to Fogg an almost certain refuge. If the warrant should at last make its appearance at Hong Kong, Fix could arrest him and give him into the hands of the local police, and there would be no further trouble. But beyond Hong Kong, a simple warrant would be of no use.

EXERCISE 1

SELF-TEST: After reading the above selection, do the following. Look at the Master Words below. Underline the words that you think you know. Circle the words that you are less sure about. Draw a square around the words you don't recognize.

MASTER WORDS

access	**picturesque**
afford	**propitious**
assert	**superb**
loom	**swarm**
panorama	**warrant**

Read the selection on the preceding page again, this time paying special attention to the ten Master Words. In the (a) spaces provided below, write down what you think is the meaning of the word. After you have attempted a definition for each word, look up the word in a dictionary. In the (b) spaces, copy the appropriate dictionary definition.

1. **access** (n.)

    a. _____

    b. _____

2. **afford** (v.)

    a. _____

    b. _____

3. **assert** (v.)

    a. _____

    b. _____

4. **loom** (v.)

    a. _____

    b. _____

5. **panorama** (n.)

    a. _____

    b. _____

6. **picturesque** (adj.)

    a. _____

    b. _____

7. **propitious** (adj.)

    a. _____

    b. _____

8. **superb** (adj.)

    a. _____

    b. _____

9. **swarm** (v.)

    a. _____

    b. _____

10. **warrant** (n.)

    a. _____

    b. _____

EXERCISE 3

Use the following list of synonyms and antonyms to fill in the blanks. Some words have no antonyms. In such cases, the antonym blanks have been marked with an X.

admission	deny	favorable	inferior	recede	unsightly
barrier	disband	gather	magnificent	rise	view
declare	document	harmful	provide	scenic	withdraw

	Synonyms	**Antonyms**
1. **propitious**	_____	_____
2. **picturesque**	_____	_____
3. **loom**	_____	_____
4. **assert**	_____	_____
5. **panorama**	_____	X
6. **superb**	_____	_____
7. **swarm**	_____	_____
8. **afford**	_____	_____
9. **access**	_____	_____
10. **warrant**	_____	X

EXERCISE 4

Decide whether the first pair in the items below are synonyms or antonyms. Then choose the Master Word that shows a similar relation to the word(s) preceding the blank.

1. fledgling	:infant	::tower	:	_____
2. prosperous	:booming	::certificate	:	_____
3. spy	:find	::fantastic	:	_____
4. homely	:luxurious	::scatter	:	_____
5. brood	:fret	::scene	:	_____
6. coax	:threaten	::ugly	:	_____
7. receptive	:willing	::entrance	:	_____
8. snug	:comfortable	::claim	:	_____
9. arrest	:prevent	::helpful	:	_____
10. shrill	:bass	::withhold	:	_____

The Master Words in this lesson are repeated below. From the Master Words, choose the appropriate word for the blank in each of the following sentences. Write the word in the numbered space provided at the right.

access	assert	panorama	propitious	swarm
afford	loom	picturesque	superb	warrant

1. The majestic white marble hall with its grand golden staircase was (a, an) ...?... example of French architecture.

1. _____

2. In the 1970s women in the United States began to ...?... their rights and demand equality as they had not done since 1920.

2. _____

3. When the rock star emerged from his dressing room, a crowd of fans ...?...(d, ed) after him to his limousine.

3. _____

4. Our game with the undefeated conference champions ...?...(d, ed) as a threat to our own successful season.

4. _____

5. Gaining ...?... to the President of the United States is no easy matter.

5. _____

6. Darcy grew fond of the simple, ...?... scene of the bridge nestled among the trees.

6. _____

7. Because they did not have (a, an) ...?..., the police officers could not search the suspect's home.

7. _____

8. We took our sailboat out into the bay when the wind seemed ...?... .

8. _____

9. The ...?... of the Battle of Gettysburg was put together from a dozen photographs found in the library.

9. _____

10. Strumming his guitar ...?...(d, ed) Denny many hours of pleasure.

10. _____

Use at least five Master Words from this lesson to write a scene about one of the following topics. Or create a topic of your own. Write your choice on the blank. Circle the Master Words as you use them.

Possible Topics: My Dream Vacation, A Photographer's Nightmare

_____

_____

_____

_____

_____

_____

_____

_____

LESSON 18

Read the following selection to get the general meaning. Read it a second time, paying special attention to the words in dark type. Notice how they are used in sentences. These are Master Words. These are the words you will be working with in this lesson.

Adapted from **Robinson Crusoe**
by Daniel Defoe

I was now landed and safe on shore, and began to look up and thank God that my life was saved in a case wherein there was some minutes before scarcely any room to hope. I believe it is impossible to express to the life what the ecstasies of the soul are when it is so saved, as I may say, out of the very grave. I walked about on the shore, lifting up my hands, reflecting upon my **deliverance**, upon all my **comrades** who were drowned. I marveled that there should not be one soul saved but myself; for, as for them, I never saw them afterwards, or any sign of them, except three of their hats, one cap, and two shoes that were not fellows.

After I had soothed my mind with the comfortable part of my condition, I began to look around me, to see what kind of place I was in, and what was next to be done; and I soon found my comforts **abate**. In a word, I had a dreadful deliverance. For I was wet, had no clothes to change to, nor anything either to eat or drink to comfort me; neither did I see any **prospect** before me, but that of **perishing** with hunger, or being devoured by wild beasts; and that which was a particular affliction to me was that I had no weapon either to hunt and kill any creature for my **sustenance**, or to defend myself against any other creatures that might desire to kill me for theirs. In a word, I had nothing about me but a knife, a tobacco pipe, and a little tobacco in a box; this was all my **provision**, and this threw me into such terrible **agonies** of mind, that for a while I ran about like a madman. Night coming upon me, I began with a heavy heart to consider what would be my lot if there were any **ravenous** beasts in that country, seeing at night they always seek their **prey**.

EXERCISE 1

SELF-TEST: After reading the above selection, do the following. Look at the Master Words below. Underline the words that you think you know. Circle the words that you are less sure about. Draw a square around the words you don't recognize.

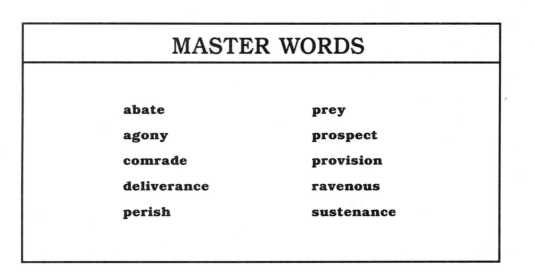

MASTER WORDS

abate	prey
agony	prospect
comrade	provision
deliverance	ravenous
perish	sustenance

Read the selection on the preceding page again, this time paying special attention to the ten Master Words. In the (a) spaces provided below, write down what you think is the meaning of the word. After you have attempted a definition for each word, look up the word in a dictionary. In the (b) spaces, copy the appropriate dictionary definition.

1. **abate** (v.)

   a. _____

   b. _____

2. **agony** (n.)

   a. _____

   b. _____

3. **comrade** (n.)

   a. _____

   b. _____

4. **deliverance** (n.)

   a. _____

   b. _____

5. **perish** (v.)

   a. _____

   b. _____

6. **prey** (n.)

   a. _____

   b. _____

7. **prospect** (n.)

   a. _____

   b. _____

8. **provision** (n.)

   a. _____

   b. _____

9. **ravenous** (adj.)

   a. _____

   b. _____

10. **sustenance** (n.)

    a. _____

    b. _____

Use the following list of synonyms and antonyms to fill in the blanks. Some words have no antonyms. In such cases, the antonym blanks have been marked with an X.

companion	ecstasy	food	improbability	predator	supply
decrease	enemy	full	increase	rescue	torment
die	expectation	hunger	live	starving	victim
downfall					

	Synonyms	**Antonyms**
1. **deliverance**	_____	_____
2. **comrade**	_____	_____
3. **abate**	_____	_____
4. **prospect**	_____	_____
5. **perish**	_____	_____
6. **sustenance**	_____	_____
7. **provision**	_____	X _____
8. **agony**	_____	_____
9. **ravenous**	_____	_____
10. **prey**	_____	_____

Decide whether the first pair in the items below are synonyms or antonyms. Then choose the Master Word that shows a similar relation to the word(s) preceding the blank.

1. warrant	:document	::possibility	: _____
2. loom	:fade	::hunter	: _____
3. swarm	:cluster	::famished	: _____
4. superb	:outstanding	::meals	: _____
5. picturesque	:disgusting	::joy	: _____
6. assert	:deny	::survive	: _____
7. afford	:supply	::associate	: _____
8. panorama	:scenery	::reduce	: _____
9. access	:passage	::stockpile	: _____
10. propitious	:beneficial	::salvation	: _____

The Master Words in this lesson are repeated below. From the Master Words, choose the appropriate word for the blank in each of the following sentences. Write the word in the numbered space provided at the right.

abate	comrade	perish	prospect	ravenous
agony	deliverance	prey	provision	sustenance

1. According to legend, St. Patrick provided ...?... for the people of Ireland when he drove the snakes from their land.

1. _____

2. After a few minutes the storm ...?...(d, ed), becoming just a mild shower.

2. _____

3. When they got home from school each afternoon, the children were ...?... and could hardly wait until dinner.

3. _____

4. A person left alone in the desert without food or water would soon ...?... .

4. _____

5. Most of the wild cats rely on short bursts of speed to bring down their ...?... .

5. _____

6. The forecaster indicated that there was little ...?... of rain.

6. _____

7. While lost in the woods, the boys ate wild fruit for ...?... .

7. _____

8. Bumping your "crazy bone" against a hard surface can be ...?... for a few seconds.

8. _____

9. Marti was in charge of packing ...?...(s) for the ten-day camping trip.

9. _____

10. Doug and his ...?...(s) organized a club for Citizens' Band radio owners in their neighborhood.

10. _____

Order the words in each item from *least* to *most*. Use the abbreviations *L* for "least" and *M* for "most." Leave the line before the word of the middle degree blank. The first word provides a clue about how to arrange the words. See the example.

dangerous: __M__treacherous   __L__questionable   ____tricky
(*Questionable* indicates the least dangerous; *treacherous* indicates the most dangerous.)

1. painful: ____agony   ____numbness   ____discomfort
2. familiar: ____acquaintance   ____stranger   ____comrade
3. deadly: ____injure   ____perish   ____cripple
4. hungry: ____ravenous   ____wanting   ____full
5. speed: ____shuffle   ____abate   ____hasten
6. necessary: ____sustenance   ____luxury   ____lodging
7. secure: ____rescue effort ____deliverance   ____danger
8. favorable: ____hopelessness   ____prospect   ____success
9. well-supplied: ____provision   ____warehouse   ____shortage
10. prized: ____prey   ____trophy   ____pest

Read the following selection to get the general meaning. Read it a second time, paying special attention to the words in dark type. Notice how they are used in sentences. These are Master Words. These are the words you will be working with in this lesson.

The Women's **Cultural** League **convened** promptly at ten o'clock Wednesday morning in the bright yellow brick meeting house on Bell Avenue. Mrs. Piddleton, a birdlike woman wearing a stiff, new pink woolen suit with black leather shoes and matching purse and hat, strutted briskly to the **podium**. She straightened her fashionable leather hat and cleared her throat to indicate the importance of beginning the official business. Silence crept into the room as the usual chatter of fashions, children, and gossip abated.

"Good morning, ladies," Mrs. Piddleton began. "Today's business concerns the plans for our new welfare program for the needy. The program will consist of a workshop set up in 'that' area, to instruct the women and their families in at least one area of culture." Mrs. Piddleton's hat wobbled as she suddenly coughed, excused herself, and continued. "Now who would like to volunteer to head this committee? It will involve much time and hard work . . ." A dainty hand edged up in the front row.

"Thank you. Anyone interested, then, please contact Mrs. Ellingsby immediately after the meeting. Refreshments will now be served in the main dining room. The meeting is **adjourned**." Mrs. Piddleton stepped down from the front of the auditorium and promptly led the way to the elegantly decorated dining area.

Down on Third Street in 14B, Charles was pouring his heart into an old, beat-up cornet in the middle of the living room. He was sprawled out on the worn carpet, tapping his foot in time to the smooth rhythm of his music. Perspiration glistened on his high forehead as he poured his soul into the horn.

Charles finished practicing and carefully placed his precious instrument in its battered, second-hand case. As he was putting the case away, he heard his sister slam the front door behind her. His mother was preparing dinner and had begun to sing. Charles was content to just sit and listen as his mother formed the soft sounds with her voice, **kneading** the cold, hard language into soothing **lyrics**. As his mother sang, Charles thought of dark molasses flowing slowly from the bottle into a mixing bowl, to be baked into something rich and delicious.

Mrs. Ellingsby interrupted the after-brunch chit-chat to announce that the "Cultural Committee for the Needy" would open their workshop two weeks **hence**. As she wiped her slender fingers on the linen napkin, she said, "Our president, Mrs. Piddleton, has graciously **consented** to **keynote** the workshop with a brief talk concerning the importance of 'Sensitivity' in the Arts.' "

—Student

EXERCISE 1

SELF-TEST: After reading the above selection, do the following. Look at the Master Words below. Underline the words that you think you know. Circle the words that you are less sure about. Draw a square around the words you don't recognize.

MASTER WORDS

adjourn	**hence**	**lyrics**
consent	**keynote**	**podium**
convene	**knead**	**sensitivity**
cultural		

Read the selection on the preceding page again, this time paying special attention to the ten Master Words. In the (a) spaces provided below, write down what you think is the meaning of the word. After you have attempted a definition for each word, look up the word in a dictionary. In the (b) spaces, copy the appropriate dictionary definition.

1. **adjourn** (v.)

    a. _____

    b. _____

2. **consent** (v.)

    a. _____

    b. _____

3. **convene** (v.)

    a. _____

    b. _____

4. **cultural** (adj.)

    a. _____

    b. _____

5. **hence** (adv.)

    a. _____

    b. _____

6. **keynote** (v.)

    a. _____

    b. _____

7. **knead** (v.)

    a. _____

    b. _____

8. **lyrics** (n.)

    a. _____

    b. _____

9. **podium** (n.)

    a. _____

    b. _____

10. **sensitivity** (n.)

    a. _____

    b. _____

Use the following list of synonyms and antonyms to fill in the blanks. Some words have no antonyms. In such cases, the antonym blanks have been marked with an X.

agree	educational	lecture	mix	prior	unawareness
crude	from now	meet	perception	recess	words
disband	gather	melody	platform	refuse	

	Synonyms	**Antonyms**
1. **cultural**	_____	_____
2. **convene**	_____	_____
3. **podium**	_____	X _____
4. **adjourn**	_____	_____
5. **knead**	_____	X _____
6. **lyrics**	_____	_____
7. **hence**	_____	_____
8. **consent**	_____	_____
9. **keynote**	_____	X _____
10. **sensitivity**	_____	_____

Decide whether the first pair in the items below are synonyms or antonyms. Then choose the Master Word that shows a similar relation to the word(s) preceding the blank.

1. prey	:attacker	::reject	: _____
2. ravenous	:satisfied	::assemble	: _____
3. prospect	:chance	::stage	: _____
4. sustenance	:nourishment	::therefore	: _____
5. agony	:delight	::tune	: _____
6. abate	:lessen	::blend	: _____
7. perish	:endure	::crudeness	: _____
8. provision	:supply	::refined	: _____
9. deliverance	:release	::address	: _____
10. comrade	:foe	::dismiss	: _____

The Master Words in this lesson are repeated below. From the Master Words, choose the appropriate word for the blank in each of the following sentences. Write the word in the numbered space provided at the right.

| adjourn | convene | hence | knead | podium |
| consent | cultural | keynote | lyrics | sensitivity |

1. Studying the ...?... contributions of a civilization gives clues to the thoughts and values of its people.

1. _____

2. The speech which ...?...(d, ed) the convention stressed the importance of economic recovery.

2. _____

3. Oscar Hammerstein II wrote ...?... for hundreds of melodies composed by Richard Rogers.

3. _____

4. In late afternoon Judge Carson ...?...(d, ed) court, ordering that everyone meet again at ten the next morning.

4. _____

5. So that the pizza crust would be tender, Jo ...?...(d, ed) the dough for ten minutes.

5. _____

6. The president suggested that speakers come to the ...?... so they could be heard.

6. _____

7. After much coaxing, Mary Lou ...?...(d, ed) to go on the choir trip in the spring.

7. _____

8. The novelist's great ...?... allowed her to realistically and powerfully capture people's emotions.

8. _____

9. The bus was late and by the time we arrived, the meeting had already ...?...(d, ed).

9. _____

10. The test is not two *days* from now but two *weeks* ...?... .

10. _____

To complete the crossword, choose the Master Word associated with each word or phrase below. Begin each answer in the square having the same number as the clue.

1. what Congress does each January
2. deliver the main speech
3. of music, drama, sculpture, for example
4. place for giving speeches
5. give your okay
6. one tuned in to others' emotions has this
7. what you may do to bread dough
8. from this day forth
9. singers belt out these
10. what you hope a dull meeting will do

LESSON 20

Read the following selection to get the general meaning. Read it a second time, paying special attention to the words in dark type. Notice how they are used in sentences. These are Master Words. These are the words you will be working with in this lesson.

From "The Man Without a Country"
by Edward Everett Hale

The rule **adopted** on board the ships on which I have met "the man without a country" was, I think, **transmitted** from the beginning. No **mess** liked to have him permanently, because his presence cut off all talk of home or of the prospect of return, of politics or letters, of peace or of war—cut off more than half the talk men like to have at sea. But it was always thought too hard that he should never meet the rest of us, except to touch hats, and we finally sank into one system. He was not permitted to talk with the men unless an officer was by. With officers he had **unrestrained** [association], as far as they and he chose. But he grew shy, though he had favorites: I was one. Then the captain always asked him to dinner on Monday. Every mess in **succession** took up the invitation in its turn. According to the size of the ship, you had him at your mess more or less often at dinner. His breakfast he ate in his own stateroom—he always had a stateroom— which was where a **sentinel**, or somebody on the watch, could see the door. And whatever else he ate or drank he ate or drank alone. Sometimes, when the marines or sailors had any special [entertainment], they were permitted to invite "Plain-Buttons," as they called him. Then Nolan was sent with some officer, and the men were forbidden to speak of home while he was there. I believe the **theory** was that the sight of his punishment did them good. They called him "Plain-Buttons" because, while he always chose to wear a **regulation** army uniform, he was not permitted to wear the army button, for the reason that it bore either the initials or the **insignia** of the country he had **disowned**.

EXERCISE 1

SELF-TEST: After reading the above selection, do the following. Look at the Master Words below. Underline the words that you think you know. Circle the words that you are less sure about. Draw a square around the words you don't recognize.

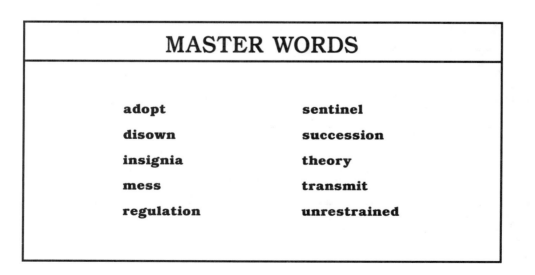

MASTER WORDS

adopt	sentinel
disown	succession
insignia	theory
mess	transmit
regulation	unrestrained

Read the selection on the preceding page again, this time paying special attention to the ten Master Words. In the (a) spaces provided below, write down what you think is the meaning of the word. After you have attempted a definition for each word, look up the word in a dictionary. In the (b) spaces, copy the appropriate dictionary definition.

1. **adopt** (v.)

   a. _____

   b. _____

2. **disown** (v.)

   a. _____

   b. _____

3. **insignia** (n.)

   a. _____

   b. _____

4. **mess** (n.)

   a. _____

   b. _____

5. **regulation** (n.)

   a. _____

   b. _____

6. **sentinel** (n.)

   a. _____

   b. _____

7. **succession** (n.)

   a. _____

   b. _____

8. **theory** (n.)

   a. _____

   b. _____

9. **transmit** (v.)

   a. _____

   b. _____

10. **unrestrained** (adj.)

   a. _____

   b. _____

Use the following list of synonyms and antonyms to fill in the blanks. Some words have no antonyms. In such cases, the antonym blanks have been marked with an X.

accept	deny	fact	idea	receive	sequence
badge	diners	free	limited	reject	unofficial
claim	disorder	guard	official	send	

	Synonyms	**Antonyms**
1. **adopt**	_____	_____
2. **transmit**	_____	_____
3. **mess**	_____	X _____
4. **unrestrained**	_____	_____
5. **succession**	_____	_____
6. **sentinel**	_____	X _____
7. **theory**	_____	_____
8. **regulation**	_____	_____
9. **insignia**	_____	X _____
10. **disown**	_____	_____

Decide whether the first pair in the items below are synonyms or antonyms. Then choose the Master Word that shows a similar relation to the word(s) preceding the blank.

1. consent	:protest	::rule out	: _____
2. podium	:stand	::eaters	: _____
3. hence	:hereafter	::steps	: _____
4. knead	:mold	::lookout	: _____
5. adjourn	:meet	::accept	: _____
6. lyrics	:musical notes	::unapproved	: _____
7. cultural	:artistic	::opinion	: _____
8. sensitivity	:awareness	::reject	: _____
9. convene	:recess	::confined	: _____
10. keynote	:speak	::symbol	: _____

The Master Words in this lesson are repeated below. From the Master Words, choose the appropriate word for the blank in each of the following sentences. Write the word in the numbered space provided at the right.

| adopt | insignia | regulation | succession | transmit |
| disown | mess | sentinel | theory | unrestrained |

1. CB radio operators ...?... messages using a lively special language.

1. _____

2. It was easy to tell where the cheerleaders were from after spotting the bold scarlet and blue ...?... on their sweaters.

2. _____

3. In classical mythology the three-headed dog Cerberus served as ...?..., guarding the gates of Hades.

3. _____

4. During the week of camp our ...?... had dining room duty for one day.

4. _____

5. The school board ...?...(d, ed) a resolution that George Washington's birthday would be a holiday on the school calendar.

5. _____

6. Although the school board hired (a, an) ...?... of coaches, not one of them was able to produce a winning team.

6. _____

7. Juanita's father threatened to ...?... her if she did not go to college and get a degree.

7. _____

8. Although Lieutenant Columbo had (a, an) ...?... about the crime, he had been unable to find evidence to support his guess.

8. _____

9. On an outing, dogs enjoy (a, an) ...?... romp off the leash.

9. _____

10. Because we did not have (a, an) ...?... court, the district tournament could not be played at our school.

10. _____

To complete the word spiral, choose the Master Word associated with each phrase below. Start with 1 and fill in each answer clockwise. Be careful! Each new word may overlap the previous word by one or more letters.

1. a coat of arms, perhaps

2. to accept a plan

3. radio or TV stations do this

4. Einstein had a famous one

5. by the book

6. wild and free

7. an angry parent might do this to a child

8. person keeping watch

9. regular mealtime group

10. just one thing after another

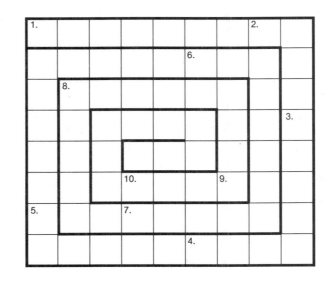

LESSON **21**

Read the following selection to get the general meaning. Read it a second time, paying special attention to the words in dark type. Notice how they are used in sentences. These are Master Words. These are the words you will be working with in this lesson.

Adapted from **"The Man Without a Country"** by Edward Everett Hale

Cape Palmas was practically as far from the homes of most of them as New Orleans or Rio de Janeiro was; that is, they would be **eternally** separated from home there. And their **interpreters**, as we could understand, instantly said, "*Ah, non Palmas,*" and began to **propose infinite** other **expedients** in most **voluble** language. Vaughan was rather disappointed at this result of his **liberality**, and asked Nolan eagerly what they said. The drops stood on poor Nolan's white forehead as he hushed the men down, and said—

"He says, 'Not Palmas.' He says, 'Take us home, take us to our own country, take us to our own house, take us to our own children and our own women.' He says he has an old father and mother who will die if they do not see him. And this one says he left his people all sick, and paddled down to Fernando to beg the white doctor to come and help them, and that these devils caught him in the bay just in sight of home, and that he has never seen anybody from home since then. And this one says," choked out Nolan, "that he has not heard a word from his home in six months, while he has been locked up in an **infernal** stockade."

Vaughan always said he grew gray himself while Nolan struggled through his interpretation. I, who did not understand anything of the passion **involved** in it, saw that the very elements were melting with **fervent** heat, and that something was to pay somewhere. Even the blacks themselves stopped howling as they saw Nolan's agony, and Vaughan's almost equal agony of sympathy. As quick as he could get words, he said—

"Tell them yes, yes, yes; tell them they shall go to the Mountains of the Moon, if they will. If I sail the schooner through the Great White Desert, they shall go home!"

EXERCISE 1

SELF-TEST: After reading the above selection, do the following. Look at the Master Words below. Underline the words that you think you know. Circle the words that you are less sure about. Draw a square around the words you don't recognize.

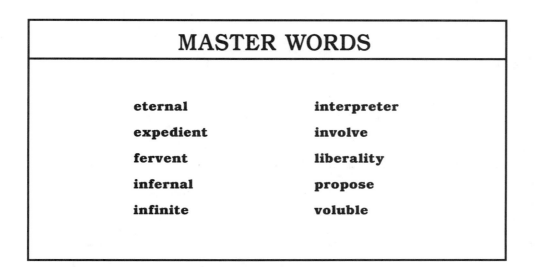

MASTER WORDS

eternal	interpreter
expedient	involve
fervent	liberality
infernal	propose
infinite	voluble

Read the selection on the preceding page again, this time paying special attention to the ten Master Words. In the (a) spaces provided below, write down what you think is the meaning of the word. After you have attempted a definition for each word, look up the word in a dictionary. In the (b) spaces, copy the appropriate dictionary definition.

1. **eternal** (adj.)

    a. _____

    b. _____

2. **expedient** (n.)

    a. _____

    b. _____

3. **fervent** (adj.)

    a. _____

    b. _____

4. **infernal** (adj.)

    a. _____

    b. _____

5. **infinite** (adj.)

    a. _____

    b. _____

6. **interpreter** (n.)

    a. _____

    b. _____

7. **involve** (v.)

    a. _____

    b. _____

8. **liberality** (n.)

    a. _____

    b. _____

9. **propose** (v.)

    a. _____

    b. _____

10. **voluble** (adj.)

    a. _____

    b. _____

Use the following list of synonyms and antonyms to fill in the blanks. Some words have no antonyms. In such cases, the antonym blanks have been marked with an X.

cold	fiery	include	quiet	stinginess	temporary
dead end	generosity	limited	recourse	suggest	translator
everlasting	heavenly	measureless	scrambler	talkative	veto
exclude	hellish				

	Synonyms	**Antonyms**
1. **eternal**	_____	_____
2. **interpreter**	_____	_____
3. **propose**	_____	_____
4. **infinite**	_____	_____
5. **expedient**	_____	_____
6. **voluble**	_____	_____
7. **liberality**	_____	_____
8. **infernal**	_____	_____
9. **involve**	_____	_____
10. **fervent**	_____	_____

Decide whether the first pair in the items below are synonyms or antonyms. Then choose the Master Word that shows a similar relation to the word(s) preceding the blank.

1. mess	:diners	::explainer	: _____
2. adopt	:veto	::short-term	: _____
3. transmit	:relay	::fluent	: _____
4. succession	:progression	::devilish	: _____
5. sentinel	:watchman	::contain	: _____
6. regulation	:unlawful	::selfishness	: _____
7. theory	:belief	::offer	: _____
8. disown	:abandon	::burning	: _____
9. unrestrained	:restricted	::barrier	: _____
10. insignia	:emblem	::boundless	: _____

The Master Words in this lesson are repeated below. From the Master Words, choose the appropriate word for the blank in each of the following sentences. Write the word in the numbered space provided at the right.

eternal	fervent	infinite	involve	propose
expedient	infernal	interpreter	liberality	voluble

1. My tormentor's ...?... grin seemed more devilish than human.

1. _____

2. Preparations for the spring carnival ...?...(d, ed) a great deal of work.

2. _____

3. The number of stars in the universe seems almost ...?... .

3. _____

4. ...?...(s) at the United Nations translate what goes on into five languages.

4. _____

5. ...?... of spirit and purse are the marks of a truly generous person.

5. _____

6. Claire's most ...?... desire was to visit England, and she saved money for years to do it.

6. _____

7. When we saw the "Road Closed" sign, we chose the ...?... and cut through Brown's pasture.

7. _____

8. Margaret ...?...(d, ed) a plan that was soon accepted by both sides.

8. _____

9. Because he was (a, an) ...?... speaker, Sandy Beach was good at his job as a disc jockey.

9. _____

10. Humans have continually sought an answer to the ageless, ...?... question: What is the meaning of life?

10. _____

Order the words in each item from *least* to *most.* Use the abbreviations *L* for "least" and *M* for "most." Leave the line before the word of the middle degree blank. The first word provides a clue about how to arrange the words. See the example.

irritation: __M__ anger ____ resentment __L__ displeasure
(*Displeasure* indicates the least irritation; *anger* indicates the most irritation.)

1. generous: ____ liberality ____ stinginess ____ economy

2. roomy: ____ vast ____ infinite ____ snug

3. hot: ____ warm ____ cool ____ fervent

4. lasting: ____ eternal ____ momentary ____ lifelong

5. pushy: ____ hint ____ demand ____ propose

6. good: ____ saintly ____ infernal ____ noble

7. progress: ____ stumbling block ____ standstill ____ expedient

8. talkative: ____ muttering ____ silent ____ voluble

9. notice: ____ involve ____ omit ____ consider

10. originality: ____ creator ____ imitator ____ interpreter

LESSON 22

Read the following selection to get the general meaning. Read it a second time, paying special attention to the words in dark type. Notice how they are used in sentences. These are Master Words. These are the words you will be working with in this lesson.

From **The Call of the Wild**
by Jack London

He had never seen dogs fight as these wolfish creatures fought, and his first experience taught him an unforgettable lesson. It is true, it was a **vicarious** experience, else he would not have lived to **profit** by it. Curly was the **victim**. They were camped near the log store, where she, in her friendly way, made advances to a husky dog the size of a full-grown wolf, though not half so large as she. There was no warning, only a leap in like a flash, a **metallic** clip of teeth, a leap out equally swift, and Curly's face was ripped open from eye to jaw.

It was the wolf manner of fighting, to strike and leap away; but there was more to it than this. Thirty or forty huskies ran to the spot and **surrounded** the **combatants** in an intent and silent circle. Buck did not [understand] that silent intentness, nor the eager way with which they were licking their chops. Curly rushed her [opponent], who struck again and leaped aside. He met her next rush with his chest, in a peculiar fashion that tumbled her off her feet. She never regained them. This was what the **onlooking** huskies had waited for. They closed in upon her, **snarling** and **yelping**, and she was buried, screaming with agony, beneath the **bristling** mass of bodies.

EXERCISE 1

SELF-TEST: After reading the above selection, do the following. Look at the Master Words below. Underline the words that you think you know. Circle the words that you are less sure about. Draw a square around the words you don't recognize.

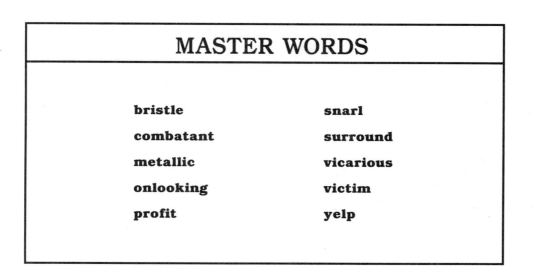

MASTER WORDS

bristle	snarl
combatant	surround
metallic	vicarious
onlooking	victim
profit	yelp

Read the selection on the preceding page again, this time paying special attention to the ten Master Words. In the (a) spaces provided below, write down what you think is the meaning of the word. After you have attempted a definition for each word, look up the word in a dictionary. In the (b) spaces, copy the appropriate dictionary definition.

1. **bristle** (v.)

   a. _____

   b. _____

2. **combatant** (n.)

   a. _____

   b. _____

3. **metallic** (adj.)

   a. _____

   b. _____

4. **onlooking** (adj.)

   a. _____

   b. _____

5. **profit** (v.)

   a. _____

   b. _____

6. **snarl** (v.)

   a. _____

   b. _____

7. **surround** (v.)

   a. _____

   b. _____

8. **vicarious** (adj.)

   a. _____

   b. _____

9. **victim** (n.)

   a. _____

   b. _____

10. **yelp** (v.)

    a. _____

    b. _____

Use the following list of synonyms and antonyms to fill in the blanks. Some words have no antonyms. In such cases, the antonym blanks have been marked with an X.

encircle	gain	metal-like	plastic	sufferer	whine
expose	growl	participating	relax	tormentor	woof
fighter	indirect	peacemaker	stiffen	watching	yap
firsthand	lose				

	Synonyms	**Antonyms**
1. **vicarious**	_____	_____
2. **profit**	_____	_____
3. **victim**	_____	_____
4. **metallic**	_____	_____
5. **surround**	_____	_____
6. **combatant**	_____	_____
7. **onlooking**	_____	_____
8. **snarl**	_____	_____
9. **yelp**	_____	_____
10. **bristle**	_____	_____

Decide whether the first pair in the items below are synonyms or antonyms. Then choose the Master Word that shows a similar relation to the word(s) preceding the blank.

1. eternal	:momentary	::retreat	: _____
2. interpreter	:encoder	::glassy	: _____
3. voluble	:silent	::torturer	: _____
4. liberality	:greed	::direct	: _____
5. infernal	:demonic	::stand up	: _____
6. involve	:concern	::bark	: _____
7. propose	:put forward	::observing	: _____
8. infinite	:endless	::cry	: _____
9. fervent	:chilly	::referee	: _____
10. expedient	:obstacle	::forfeit	: _____

The Master Words in this lesson are repeated below. From the Master Words, choose the appropriate word for the blank in each of the following sentences. Write the word in the numbered space provided at the right.

bristle	metallic	profit	surround	victim
combatant	onlooking	snarl	vicarious	yelp

1. Although our experience was only ...?..., our neighbors' slides made us feel as if we, too, had enjoyed a vacation in Hawaii.

1. _____

2. When strangers approach, Bowser begins to ...?... angrily.

2. _____

3. Since she had been able to visit Congress for a day, Doris felt she had greatly ...?...(d, ed) from her trip to Washington.

3. _____

4. The referee ordered the two ...?...(s) to come from their corners fighting at the sound of the bell.

4. _____

5. The crewcut made Jason's hair ...?... and stand up stiffly.

5. _____

6. The ...?... crowd cheered as the baton was passed to the last runner on the relay team.

6. _____

7. Although (a, an) ...?... of polio, Franklin D. Roosevelt led a full life as President of the United States.

7. _____

8. Troops ...?...(d, ed) the enemy, cutting off all possible means of retreat.

8. _____

9. Until Nate put a clock in the lonesome puppy's bed, it ...?...(d, ed) and whined for its mother.

9. _____

10. Gold glitter gave (a, an) ...?... appearance to the vase the child had decorated for Mother's Day.

10. _____

Fill in the chart below with the Master Word that fits each set of clues. Part of speech refers to the word's usage in the lesson. Use a dictionary when necessary.

Number of Syllables	Part of Speech	Other Clues	Master Word
1	verb	a grouch may make this sound	1. _____
3	adjective	like the sound of a hammer against an anvil	2. _____
2	noun	the injured party	3. _____
4	adjective	type of experience soap operas provide	4. _____
2	verb	an angry cat's fur does this	5. _____
3	adjective	a crowd at an accident is this way	6. _____
2	verb	what a fence does to a yard	7. _____
3	noun	not a peacemaker	8. _____
1	verb	cry in pain	9. _____
2	verb	owners hope business will do this	10. _____

LESSON 23

Read the following selection to get the general meaning. Read it a second time, paying special attention to the words in dark type. Notice how they are used in sentences. These are Master Words. These are the words you will be working with in this lesson.

From **"The Bottle Imp"**
by Robert Louis Stevenson

The house was all brand new, and the trees in the garden no greater than walking-sticks, and the lawyer, when he came, had the **air** of a man well pleased.

"What can I do to serve you?" said the lawyer.

"You are a friend of Lopaka's," replied Keawe, "and Lopaka purchased from me a certain piece of goods that I thought you might **enable** me to **trace**."

The lawyer's face became very dark. "I do not **profess** to misunderstand you, Mr. Keawe," said he, "though this is an ugly business to be stirring in. You may be sure I know nothing, but yet I have a guess, and if you would **apply** in a certain **quarter** I think you might have news."

And he named the name of a man, which, again, I had better not repeat. So it was for days, and Keawe went from one to another, finding everywhere new clothes and carriages, and fine new houses and men everywhere in great **contentment**, although, to be sure, when he hinted at his business their faces would cloud over.

"No doubt I am upon the track," thought Keawe. "These new clothes and carriages are all the gifts of the little imp, and these glad faces are the faces of men who have taken their profit and got rid of the **accursed** thing in safety. When I see pale cheeks and hear sighing, I shall know that I am near the bottle."

So it befell at last [that a place in Beritania Street was **recommended** to him]. When he came to the door, about the hour of the evening meal, there were the usual marks of the new house, and the young garden, and the electric light shining in the windows; but when the owner came, a shock of hope and fear ran through Keawe; for here was a young man, white as a corpse, and black about the eyes, the hair shedding from his head, and such a look in his countenance as a man may have when he is waiting for the **gallows**.

EXERCISE 1

SELF-TEST: After reading the above selection, do the following. Look at the Master Words below. Underline the words that you think you know. Circle the words that you are less sure about. Draw a square around the words you don't recognize.

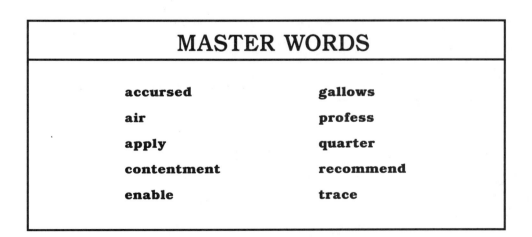

MASTER WORDS

accursed	gallows
air	profess
apply	quarter
contentment	recommend
enable	trace

Read the selection on the preceding page again, this time paying special attention to the ten Master Words. In the (a) spaces provided below, write down what you think is the meaning of the word. After you have attempted a definition for each word, look up the word in a dictionary. In the (b) spaces, copy the appropriate dictionary definition.

1. **accursed** (adj.)

   a. _____

   b. _____

2. **air** (n.)

   a. _____

   b. _____

3. **apply** (v.)

   a. _____

   b. _____

4. **contentment** (n.)

   a. _____

   b. _____

5. **enable** (v.)

   a. _____

   b. _____

6. **gallows** (n.)

   a. _____

   b. _____

7. **profess** (v.)

   a. _____

   b. _____

8. **quarter** (n.)

   a. _____

   b. _____

9. **recommend** (v.)

   a. _____

   b. _____

10. **trace** (v.)

   a. _____

   b. _____

Use the following list of synonyms and antonyms to fill in the blanks. Some words have no antonyms. In such cases, the antonym blanks have been marked with an X.

allow	damned	lose	prevent	satisfaction	supply
blessed	deny	manner	reject	scaffold	track
claim	district	misery	request	suggest	

	Synonyms	**Antonyms**
1. **air**	_____	X _____
2. **enable**	_____	_____
3. **trace**	_____	_____
4. **profess**	_____	_____
5. **apply**	_____	_____
6. **quarter**	_____	X _____
7. **contentment**	_____	_____
8. **accursed**	_____	_____
9. **recommend**	_____	_____
10. **gallows**	_____	X _____

Decide whether the first pair in the items below are synonyms or antonyms. Then choose the Master Word that shows a similar relation to the word(s) preceding the blank.

1. surround	:enclose	::doomed	: _____
2. victim	:bully	::furnish	: _____
3. metallic	:metal-like	::hanging platform	: _____
4. vicarious	:personal	::unhappiness	: _____
5. combatant	:competitor	::trail	: _____
6. bristle	:stiffen	::appearance	: _____
7. snarl	:snap	::zone	: _____
8. profit	:benefit	::offer	: _____
9. onlooking	:contributing	::interfere	: _____
10. yelp	:howl	::state	: _____

The Master Words in this lesson are repeated below. From the Master Words, choose the appropriate word for the blank in each of the following sentences. Write the word in the numbered space provided at the right.

accursed	apply	enable	profess	recommend
air	contentment	gallows	quarter	trace

1. When Lois realized that her package had not been received, she asked the post office to ...?... it.

1. _____

2. Many students and artists live in that ...?... of the city.

2. _____

3. Although Annette ...?...(d, ed) to be a close friend of the singer, he apparently had no recollection of her.

3. _____

4. Scholarships ...?... many deserving students to pursue a college education which they otherwise could not afford.

4. _____

5. In some states the gas chamber or the electric chair replaced the ...?... as a means of execution.

5. _____

6. The guitarist gave the stuffy concert a fresh, modern ...?... .

6. _____

7. After Fred lost his student identification card, he had to ...?... for a new one through student services.

7. _____

8. The doctor ...?...(d, ed) a regular exercise program for most of his patients.

8. _____

9. Ignorance during colonial times led to a belief that epilepsy victims were ...?..., and they were labeled as witches.

9. _____

10. ...?... is best known to sleeping children and well-fed dogs.

10. _____

The invented words below are formed from parts of different Master Words from this lesson. Create a definition and indicate the part of speech for each word. The first one is done for you.

traceair _(adj.) the appearance or look of a detective_ _____

gallowfess _____

quartertrace _____

recommentment _____

Now invent your own words by combining parts of the Master Words. Create a definition for each, and indicate the word's part of speech. (You may reuse any of the word parts above in new combinations.)

1. _____ _____

2. _____ _____

LESSON 24

PART I: From the list below, choose the appropriate word for each sentence that follows. Use each word only once. There will be two words left over.

access	exchange	loom	prospect	sensitivity
breach	insignificant	panorama	receptive	trace
counsel	interpreter	picturesque	relative	

1. When Kay _____(d, ed) her family tree, she discovered that one of her great-great aunts had been an American Indian.

2. Because each of the two boys found the other's sandwich more appetizing, they decided to _____ lunches.

3. The Panama Canal provides _____ to the Atlantic Ocean from the Pacific Ocean.

4. Because my company moved from our office before the lease ran out, the landlord threatened to sue us for _____ of contract.

5. Before Brent made a decision, he sought the _____ and opinion of his friend.

6. Because of the _____ of their skin, some people must use a very gentle soap or wear special, soft clothing.

7. The view from the mountain was a superb _____ offering glimpses of four states.

8. To a five-year-old, forty seems old, but to a seventy-year-old, forty seems young; age is one thing that is _____.

9. Although officials said that the _____ for an economic recovery was good, unemployment and the cost of living continued to rise.

10. While some groups are _____ to new members, others do not quickly welcome strangers.

11. The committee members agreed to ignore _____ details and just concentrate on the important points.

12. Calculus is almost a foreign language to me, and I wish I knew (a, an) _____ who could explain it in simple terms.

PART II: Decide whether the first pair in the items below are synonyms or antonyms. Then choose a Master Word from Lessons 13-23 which shows a similar relation to the word(s) preceding the blank. Do not repeat a Master Word that appears in the first column.

1. propose   :recommend   ::opinion   : _____

2. afford   :contribute   ::patrol   : _____

3. comrade   :rival   ::heartbreak   : _____

4. warrant   :credential   ::assemble   : _____

5. arrest   :curb   ::gain   : _____

91   LESSON TWENTY-FOUR

PART III: From the list below, choose the appropriate word for each sentence that follows. Use each word only once. There will be two words left over.

adjourn	incredible	merely	recommend	transmit
disown	infinite	overtake	regulation	vicarious
enable	involve	prosperous	subtle	

1. Some common diseases are _____(d, ed) by coughing or sneezing.

2. When Mitch became a football star, his father _____ (ly) fulfilled his own boyhood dream of stardom.

3. So _____ was the interviewer in obtaining information, we did not realize we had told him more than we had intended.

4. To make sure that our baskets were _____ height, we checked three rule books.

5. Although Mr. Taylor's business had a slow beginning, today it is one of the most secure and _____ in the city.

6. Dr. Davis _____(d, ed) that Pete move to a warm, dry climate where his asthma would be easier to control.

7. That someone had actually survived on a life raft for twenty-eight days seemed absolutely _____.

8. Since his bike was not equipped with a headlight, Jim hoped that darkness would not _____ him before he reached home.

9. The rising young star promptly _____(d, ed) his old associates and refused to even mention their names.

10. Some people believe that fate is fixed, but I think the possibilities in life are as _____ as time.

11. The meeting will begin at three and probably _____ before five.

12. Selling these five hundred boxes of oranges will _____ our choir to go on a trip.

PART IV: Decide whether the first pair in the items below are synonyms or antonyms. Then choose a Master Word from Lessons 13-23 which shows a similar relation to the word(s) preceding the blank. Do not repeat a Master Word that appears in the first column.

1. reflect :think over ::scold : _____

2. astonishment :surprise ::strange : _____

3. snug :secure ::declare : _____

4. sensitivity :unawareness ::brief : _____

5. contempt :favor ::grow : _____

LESSON 25

Read the following selection to get the general meaning. Read it a second time, paying special attention to the words in dark type. Notice how they are used in sentences. These are Master Words. These are the words you will be working with in this lesson.

Adapted from **"The Bottle Imp"**
by Robert Louis Stevenson

"Here it is, to be sure," thought Keawe, and so with this man he did nothing to **veil** his **errand**. "I am come to buy the bottle," said he.

At the word, the young man of Beritania Street **reeled** against the wall.

"The bottle!" he **gasped**. "To buy the bottle!" Then he seemed to choke, and **seizing** Keawe by the arm, [**conducted**] him into a room and poured out wine in two glasses.

"Here are my **respects**," said Keawe, who had been much about in his time. "Yes," he added, "I am come to buy the bottle. What is the price by now?"

At that word the young man let his glass slip through his fingers, and looked upon Keawe like a ghost.

"The price," says he; "the price! You do not know the price?"

"It is for that I am asking you," returned Keawe. "But why are you so much **concerned**? Is there anything wrong about the price?"

"It has dropped a great deal in value since your time, Mr. Keawe," said the young man, **stammering**.

"Well, well, I shall have the less to pay for it," says Keawe. "How much did it cost you?"

The young man was as white as a sheet. "Two cents," said he.

"What?" cried Keawe, "two cents? Why, then, you can only sell it for one. And he who buys it—" The words died upon Keawe's tongue; he who bought it could never sell it again, the bottle and the bottle imp must **abide** with him until he died, and when he died must carry him to the red end of hell.

EXERCISE 1

SELF-TEST: After reading the above selection, do the following. Look at the Master Words below. Underline the words that you think you know. Circle the words that you are less sure about. Draw a square around the words you don't recognize.

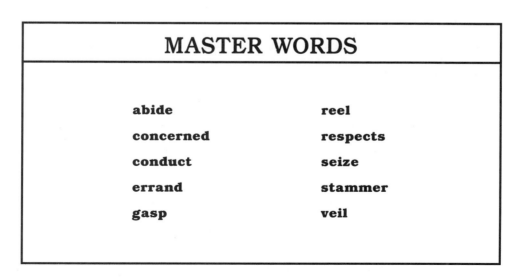

MASTER WORDS

abide	**reel**
concerned	**respects**
conduct	**seize**
errand	**stammer**
gasp	**veil**

93

LESSON TWENTY-FIVE

Read the selection on the preceding page again, this time paying special attention to the ten Master Words. In the (a) spaces provided below, write down what you think is the meaning of the word. After you have attempted a definition for each word, look up the word in a dictionary. In the (b) spaces, copy the appropriate dictionary definition.

1. **abide** (v.)

    a. _____

    b. _____

2. **concerned** (adj.)

    a. _____

    b. _____

3. **conduct** (v.)

    a. _____

    b. _____

4. **errand** (n.)

    a. _____

    b. _____

5. **gasp** (v.)

    a. _____

    b. _____

6. **reel** (v.)

    a. _____

    b. _____

7. **respects** (n.)

    a. _____

    b. _____

8. **seize** (v.)

    a. _____

    b. _____

9. **stammer** (v.)

    a. _____

    b. _____

10. **veil** (v.)

    a. _____

    b. _____

Use the following list of synonyms and antonyms to fill in the blanks. Some words have no antonyms. In such cases, the antonym blanks have been marked with an X.

anxious	go	pant	release	ridicule	stutter
conceal	grab	pronounce	relieved	stagger	task
follow	lead	regards	reveal	stay	walk

	Synonyms	**Antonyms**
1. **veil**	_____	_____
2. **errand**	_____	X
3. **reel**	_____	_____
4. **gasp**	_____	X
5. **seize**	_____	_____
6. **conduct**	_____	_____
7. **respects**	_____	_____
8. **concerned**	_____	_____
9. **stammer**	_____	_____
10. **abide**	_____	_____

Decide whether the first pair in the items below are synonyms or antonyms. Then choose the Master Word that shows a similar relation to the word(s) preceding the blank.

1. accursed	:favored	::expose	: _____
2. gallows	:scaffold	::clutch	: _____
3. apply	:seek	::remain	: _____
4. contentment	:restlessness	::glide	: _____
5. air	:expression	::wheeze	: _____
6. quarter	:area	::hesitate	: _____
7. recommend	:suggest	::duty	: _____
8. profess	:pretend to	::guide	: _____
9. trace	:misplace	::carefree	: _____
10. enable	:block	::insults	: _____

The Master Words in this lesson are repeated below. From the Master Words, choose the appropriate word for the blank in each of the following sentences. Write the word in the numbered space provided at the right.

| abide | conduct | gasp | respects | stammer |
| concerned | errand | reel | seize | veil |

1. "Give my ...?... to the old chap," Wilson said when I told him I was going to visit our beloved schoolmaster, Mr. Chips.

1. _____

2. Not particularly ...?... when the child threatened to run away from home, his parents offered to help him pack.

2. _____

3. The force of the blow caused Al to ...?... across the room.

3. _____

4. Although it is said he ...?...(d, ed) as a youth, Demosthenes later became a great speaker and statesman in ancient Athens.

4. _____

5. Because Luke could ...?... a ball so quickly from opponents, he was nicknamed "Grab Hands."

5. _____

6. Dolores mailed the letters and delivered the dry cleaning, but she forgot the other ...?... her mother had asked her to do.

6. _____

7. Although Hugh's criticism was ...?...(d, ed) in laughter, everyone believed it to be a true expression of his feelings.

7. _____

8. Because the play had already started when we arrived, the usher used a flashlight to ...?... us to our seats.

8. _____

9. Renee ...?...(d, ed) when she saw that the dress she had casually admired cost $300.

9. _____

10. I doubted that Juan, who had lived in the city most of his life, would long ...?... in our sleepy town.

10. _____

To complete the word spiral, choose the Master Word associated with each phrase below. Start with 1 and fill in each answer clockwise. Be careful! Each new word may overlap the previous word by one or more letters.

1. tour guides do this

2. to cover up

3. do this to an opportunity

4. you pay these to people you admire

5. stumble over words

6. you may do this when punched

7. stay in a place

8. a person may have to "run" one of these

9. breathless reaction

10. your attitude before a big test, perhaps

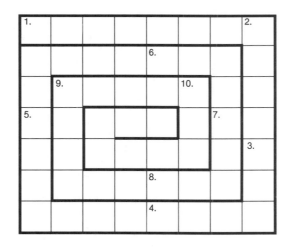

LESSON 26

Read the following selection to get the general meaning. Read it a second time, paying special attention to the words in dark type. Notice how they are used in sentences. These are Master Words. These are the words you will be working with in this lesson.

From **The Red Pony**
by John Steinbeck

The night was very dark and far-off noises carried in clearly. The harness bells of a wood team sounded from way over the hill on the county road. Jody picked his way across the dark yard. He could see a light through the window of the little room of the bunkhouse. Because the night was secret he walked quietly up to the window and **peered** in. Gitano sat in the rocking-chair and his back was toward the window. His right arm moved slowly back and forth in front of him. Jody pushed the door open and walked in. Gitano jerked upright and, seizing a piece of deerskin, he tried to throw it over the thing in his lap, but the skin slipped away. Jody stood **overwhelmed** by the thing in Gitano's hand, a **lean** and lovely **rapier** with a golden basket **hilt**. The blade was like a thin ray of dark light. The hilt was pierced and **intricately** carved.

"What is it?" Jody demanded.

Gitano only looked at him with **resentful** eyes, and he picked up the fallen deerskin and firmly wrapped the beautiful blade in it.

Jody put out his hand. "Can't I see it?"

Gitano's eyes **smoldered** angrily and he shook his head.

"Where'd you get it? Where'd it come from?"

Now Gitano regarded him **profoundly**, as though he **pondered**. "I got it from my father."

"Well, where'd he get it?"

Gitano looked down at the long deerskin parcel in his hand. "I don't know."

"Didn't he ever tell you?"

"No."

"What do you do with it?"

Gitano looked slightly surprised. "Nothing. I just keep it."

"Can't I see it again?"

The old man slowly unwrapped the shining blade and let the lamplight slip along it for a moment. Then he wrapped it up again. "You go now. I want to go to bed." He blew out the lamp almost before Jody had closed the door.

—Copyright 1937, 1938 by John Steinbeck.
Reprinted by permission of The Viking Press, Inc.

EXERCISE 1

SELF-TEST: After reading the above selection, do the following. Look at the Master Words below. Underline the words that you think you know. Circle the words that you are less sure about. Draw a square around the words you don't recognize.

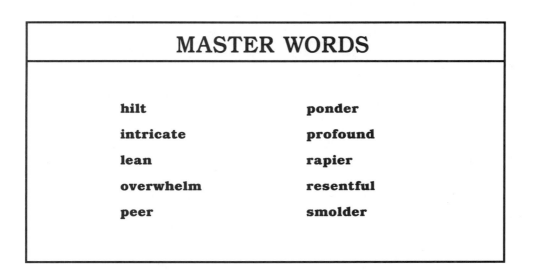

MASTER WORDS	
hilt	ponder
intricate	profound
lean	rapier
overwhelm	resentful
peer	smolder

Read the selection on the preceding page again, this time paying special attention to the ten Master Words. In the (a) spaces provided below, write down what you think is the meaning of the word. After you have attempted a definition for each word, look up the word in a dictionary. In the (b) spaces, copy the appropriate dictionary definition.

1. **hilt** (n.)

    a. _____

    b. _____

2. **intricate** (adj.)

    a. _____

    b. _____

3. **lean** (adj.)

    a. _____

    b. _____

4. **overwhelm** (v.)

    a. _____

    b. _____

5. **peer** (v.)

    a. _____

    b. _____

6. **ponder** (v.)

    a. _____

    b. _____

7. **profound** (adj.)

    a. _____

    b. _____

8. **rapier** (n.)

    a. _____

    b. _____

9. **resentful** (adj.)

    a. _____

    b. _____

10. **smolder** (v.)

    a. _____

    b. _____

Use the following list of synonyms and antonyms to fill in the blanks. Some words have no antonyms. In such cases, the antonym blanks have been marked with an X.

angry	deep	ignore	plump	smoke
blaze	forgiving	overpower	shallow	sword
complicated	gaze	peek	simple	thin
consider	handle			

	Synonyms	**Antonyms**
1. **peer**	_____	_____
2. **overwhelm**	_____	X
3. **lean**	_____	_____
4. **rapier**	_____	X
5. **hilt**	_____	X
6. **intricate**	_____	_____
7. **resentful**	_____	_____
8. **smolder**	_____	_____
9. **profound**	_____	_____
10. **ponder**	_____	_____

Decide whether the first pair in the items below are synonyms or antonyms. Then choose the Master Word that shows a similar relation to the word(s) preceding the blank.

1. seize	:grasp	::blade	: _____
2. gasp	:gulp	::defeat	: _____
3. veil	:uncover	::fat	: _____
4. abide	:leave	::unimportant	: _____
5. stammer	:stutter	::stare	: _____
6. reel	:skate	::grateful	: _____
7. errand	:chore	::reflect	: _____
8. concerned	:unworried	::flame	: _____
9. respects	:scorn	::uncomplicated	: _____
10. conduct	:direct	::grip	: _____

The Master Words in this lesson are repeated below. From the Master Words, choose the appropriate word for the blank in each of the following sentences. Write the word in the numbered space provided at the right.

hilt	lean	peer	profound	resentful
intricate	overwhelm	ponder	rapier	smolder

1. The soldier ...?...(d, ed) through the branches of the tree, waiting to catch sight of the enemy.

1. _____

2. The careful, ...?... details of the painter's work could only be appreciated after long and close study.

2. _____

3. The generosity of their neighbors ...?...(d, ed) the family whose home had been destroyed by fire.

3. _____

4. Marlene ...?...(d, ed) her choices before making her decision.

4. _____

5. Philip Nolan developed (a, an) ...?... love for the country that he had recklessly disowned many years earlier.

5. _____

6. As the clown prepared to draw his sword, the ...?... slipped off in his hand, leaving the blade in the sheath.

6. _____

7. Grace could not help feeling ...?... toward her older sister because of the special privileges Carrie was given.

7. _____

8. Although (a, an) ...?... man, Tony was strong and healthy.

8. _____

9. John bought an old ...?... that had supposedly been used in hand-to-hand combat during the sixteenth century.

9. _____

10. Anger allowed to ...?... within is usually more harmful than anger that is expressed.

10. _____

To complete this puzzle, fill in the Master Word associated with each phrase below. Then unscramble the circled letters to form a Master Word from Lesson 25, and define it.

1. a deep thought can be this way

— — — — — — — — —

2. it is double-edged

— — — — — — —

3. what a surprise may do

— — — — — — ⊙ — —

4. an angry person or a fire may do this

— ⊙ — — — — — —

5. like the plot of a complex mystery

— — — — — ⊙ — —

6. to look through binoculars

— — — — ⊙ — —

7. how you might feel if you're left out

— — ⊙ — — — — — —

8. to pick up a knife, you'd grasp this

— — — — ⊙

9. most marathon runners are this way

— — ⊙ — —

10. think it over

— — — — — ⊙

Unscrambled word: _____

Definition: _____

LESSON 27

Read the following selection to get the general meaning. Read it a second time, paying special attention to the words in dark type. Notice how they are used in sentences. These are Master Words. These are the words you will be working with in this lesson.

From **The Red Badge of Courage**
by Stephen Crane

The youth **cringed** as if discovered in a crime. By heavens, they had won after all!

. . . .

He turned away amazed and angry. He felt that he had been wronged.

He had fled, he told himself, because **annihilation** approached. He had done a good part in saving himself, who was a little piece of the army. He had considered the time, he said, to be one in which it was the duty of every little piece to rescue itself if possible. Later the officers could fit the little pieces together again, and make a battle front. If none of the little pieces were wise enough to save themselves from the flurry of death at such a time, why, then, where would be the army? It was all plain that he had proceeded according to very correct and **commendable** rules. His actions had been **sagacious** things. They had been full of **strategy**. They were the work of a master's legs.

Thoughts of his comrades came to him. The **brittle** blue line had withstood the blows and won. He grew bitter over it. It seemed that the blind ignorance and stupidity of those little pieces had **betrayed** him. He had been overturned and crushed by their lack of sense in holding the position, when intelligent **deliberation** would have convinced them that it was impossible. He, the **enlightened** man who looks afar in the dark, had fled because of his **superior** perceptions and knowledge. He felt a great anger against his comrades. He knew it could be proved that they had been fools.

EXERCISE 1

SELF-TEST: After reading the above selection, do the following. Look at the Master Words below. Underline the words that you think you know. Circle the words that you are less sure about. Draw a square around the words you don't recognize.

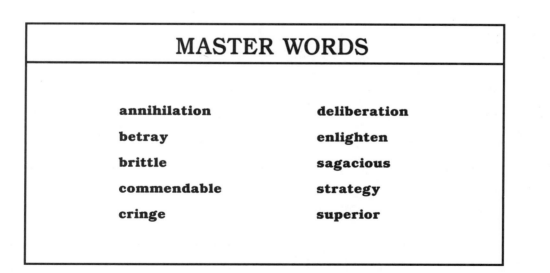

MASTER WORDS

annihilation	deliberation
betray	enlighten
brittle	sagacious
commendable	strategy
cringe	superior

Read the selection on the preceding page again, this time paying special attention to the ten Master Words. In the (a) spaces provided below, write down what you think is the meaning of the word. After you have attempted a definition for each word, look up the word in a dictionary. In the (b) spaces, copy the appropriate dictionary definition.

1. **annihilation** (n.)

    a. _____

    b. _____

2. **betray** (v.)

    a. _____

    b. _____

3. **brittle** (adj.)

    a. _____

    b. _____

4. **commendable** (adj.)

    a. _____

    b. _____

5. **cringe** (v.)

    a. _____

    b. _____

6. **deliberation** (n.)

    a. _____

    b. _____

7. **enlighten** (v.)

    a. _____

    b. _____

8. **sagacious** (adj.)

    a. _____

    b. _____

9. **strategy** (n.)

    a. _____

    b. _____

10. **superior** (adj.)

    a. _____

    b. _____

Use the following list of synonyms and antonyms to fill in the blanks. Some words have no antonyms. In such cases, the antonym blanks have been marked with an X.

confront	destruction	excellent	impulsiveness	scheme	sturdy
confuse	disgusting	foolish	inform	second-rate	support
cower	double-cross	fragile	praiseworthy	study	wise
creation					

	Synonyms	**Antonyms**
1. **cringe**	_____	_____
2. **annihilation**	_____	_____
3. **commendable**	_____	_____
4. **sagacious**	_____	_____
5. **strategy**	_____	X _____
6. **brittle**	_____	_____
7. **betray**	_____	_____
8. **deliberation**	_____	_____
9. **enlighten**	_____	_____
10. **superior**	_____	_____

Decide whether the first pair in the items below are synonyms or antonyms. Then choose the Master Word that shows a similar relation to the word(s) preceding the blank.

1. rapier	:sword	::plan	: _____
2. ponder	:gloss over	::strong	: _____
3. profound	:trivial	::displeasing	: _____
4. overwhelm	:overcome	::tremble	: _____
5. resentful	:bitter	::two-time	: _____
6. peer	:watch	::death	: _____
7. smolder	:blaze	::ignorant	: _____
8. lean	:overweight	::perplex	: _____
9. intricate	:straightforward	::low-grade	: _____
10. hilt	:holder	::consideration	: _____

The Master Words in this lesson are repeated below. From the Master Words, choose the appropriate word for the blank in each of the following sentences. Write the word in the numbered space provided at the right.

annihilation   brittle   cringe   enlighten   strategy
betray   commendable   deliberation   sagacious   superior

1. Sherlock Holmes, a particularly brilliant, ...?... detective, deduced facts from easily missed clues.

1. _____

2. A person's bones become more ...?... with age and are inclined to break more easily.

2. _____

3. It is estimated that six million Jews were killed by Nazis after Hitler ordered their ...?... .

3. _____

4. The Trojan Horse, filled with armed Greeks and taken into Troy, was the ...?... that turned the tide of the Trojan War.

4. _____

5. Although the eighth graders did not defeat the ninth graders in the softball game, they made (a, an) ...?... effort.

5. _____

6. The jury spent twelve hours in ...?... before delivering a verdict of "not guilty."

6. _____

7. I agreed to give Kurt a second chance after he swore he would never ...?... my trust again.

7. _____

8. William Harvey ...?...(d, ed) the world as to how blood flows through the human body.

8. _____

9. The very mention of the word "snake" is enough to make some people ...?... and turn pale.

9. _____

10. A porterhouse steak is generally regarded as a fine, ...?... cut of beef.

10. _____

To complete the crossword, choose the Master Word associated with each word or phrase below. Begin each answer in the square having the same number as the clue.

1. a wise person might be called this

2. Benedict Arnold did this

3. the task of a jury weighing evidence

4. stiff but easily broken

5. widespread destruction

6. what a mouse may do when a cat is nearby

7. to throw some light on the subject

8. a grade of A, for example

9. what a military leader may follow

10. deserves a pat on the back

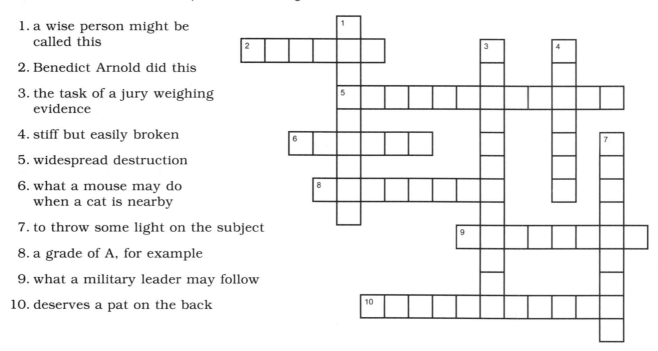

Read the following selection to get the general meaning. Read it a second time, paying special attention to the words in dark type. Notice how they are used in sentences. These are Master Words. These are the words you will be working with in this lesson.

Adapted from **"To Build a Fire"**
by Jack London

The old-timer on Sulphur Creek was right, he thought in the moment of controlled despair that **ensued**: after fifty below, a man should travel with a partner. He beat his hands, but failed in exciting any **sensation**. Suddenly he bared both hands, removing the mittens with his teeth. He caught the whole bunch of matches between the heels of his hands. His arm muscles not being frozen enabled him to press the hand heels tightly against the matches. Then he scratched the bunch along his leg. It burst into flame, seventy sulphur matches at once! There was no wind to blow them out. He kept his head to one side to escape the **strangling fumes**, and held the blazing bunch to the birch bark. As he so held it, he became aware of sensation in his hand. His flesh was burning. He could smell it. Deep down below the surface he could feel it. The sensation developed into pain that grew **acute**.

At last, when he could stand no more, he jerked his hands apart. The blazing matches fell **sizzling** into the snow, but the birch bark was alight. He began laying dry grasses and the tiniest twigs on the flame. He could not pick and choose, for he had to lift the fuel between the heels of his hands. Small pieces of rotten wood and green moss clung to the twigs, and he bit them off as well as he could with his teeth. He **cherished** the flame carefully and awkwardly. It meant life, and it must not perish. As blood withdrew from the surface of his body he began to shiver, and he grew more awkward. A large piece of green moss fell directly on the little fire. He tried to poke it out with his fingers, but his shivering frame made him poke too far, and he **disrupted** the **nucleus** of the little fire, the burning grasses and tiny twigs separating and scattering. He tried to poke them together again, but in spite of the tenseness of the effort, his shivering got away with him, and the twigs were hopelessly scattered. Each twig **gushed** a puff of smoke and went out. The fire provider had failed.

—From "To Build a Fire" from Lost Face *by Jack London. Used by permission.*

EXERCISE 1

SELF-TEST: After reading the above selection, do the following. Look at the Master Words below. Underline the words that you think you know. Circle the words that you are less sure about. Draw a square around the words you don't recognize.

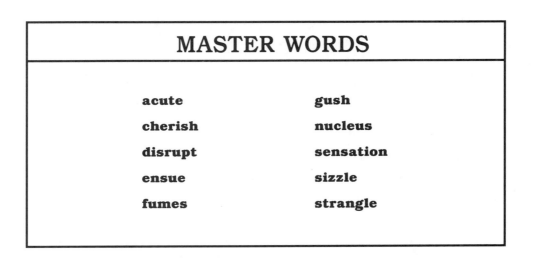

MASTER WORDS

acute	**gush**
cherish	**nucleus**
disrupt	**sensation**
ensue	**sizzle**
fumes	**strangle**

Read the selection on the preceding page again, this time paying special attention to the ten Master Words. In the (a) spaces provided below, write down what you think is the meaning of the word. After you have attempted a definition for each word, look up the word in a dictionary. In the (b) spaces, copy the appropriate dictionary definition.

1. **acute** (adj.)

   a. _____

   b. _____

2. **cherish** (v.)

   a. _____

   b. _____

3. **disrupt** (v.)

   a. _____

   b. _____

4. **ensue** (v.)

   a. _____

   b. _____

5. **fumes** (n.)

   a. _____

   b. _____

6. **gush** (v.)

   a. _____

   b. _____

7. **nucleus** (n.)

   a. _____

   b. _____

8. **sensation** (n.)

   a. _____

   b. _____

9. **sizzle** (v.)

   a. _____

   b. _____

10. **strangle** (v.)

   a. _____

   b. _____

EXERCISE 3

Use the following list of synonyms and antonyms to fill in the blanks. Some words have no antonyms. In such cases, the antonym blanks have been marked with an X.

center	disturb	feeling	harmonize	pour	sharp
choke	dull	follow	hiss	precede	trickle
despise	edge	gas	numbness	revive	value

	Synonyms	**Antonyms**
1. **ensue**	_____	_____
2. **sensation**	_____	_____
3. **strangle**	_____	_____
4. **fumes**	_____	X
5. **acute**	_____	_____
6. **sizzle**	_____	X
7. **cherish**	_____	_____
8. **disrupt**	_____	_____
9. **nucleus**	_____	_____
10. **gush**	_____	_____

EXERCISE 4

Decide whether the first pair in the items below are synonyms or antonyms. Then choose the Master Word that shows a similar relation to the word(s) preceding the blank.

1. brittle	:unbreakable	::balance	: _____
2. commendable	:offensive	::weak	: _____
3. strategy	:tactics	::core	: _____
4. cringe	:shrink	::smoke	: _____
5. betray	:befriend	::drip	: _____
6. annihilation	:slaughter	::touch	: _____
7. enlighten	:educate	::fizz	: _____
8. deliberation	:reflection	::smother	: _____
9. sagacious	:stupid	::go before	: _____
10. superior	:average	::neglect	: _____

The Master Words in this lesson are repeated below. From the Master Words, choose the appropriate word for the blank in each of the following sentences. Write the word in the numbered space provided at the right.

acute	disrupt	fumes	nucleus	sizzle
cherish	ensue	gush	sensation	strangle

1. Excitement sprang up across Oklahoma in the 1920s as oil ...?...(d, ed) from the ground at one site after another.

1. _____

2. The ...?... of my huge library is a set of encyclopedias and the Harvard Classics.

2. _____

3. A ventilator helped remove the cooking ...?... from the kitchen.

3. _____

4. Our appetites grew as we heard the hamburgers ...?... on the grill.

4. _____

5. A noisy, rude drunk ...?...(d, ed) our quiet party.

5. _____

6. Lois finally went to the doctor when the dull ache in her back became (a, an) ...?... pain.

6. _____

7. Randy ...?...(d, ed) the old paperweights because they had been collected by his parents.

7. _____

8. After the principal's lecture expressing his contempt for cheaters, a tense silence ...?...(d, ed).

8. _____

9. Sally nearly ...?...(d, ed) when a piece of food stuck in her windpipe.

9. _____

10. Taking a warm shower after a tough workout provides a pleasant, soothing ...?... .

10. _____

Write the Master Word that is associated with each word group below. Then list three things that might be associated with the review word that follows.

1. power failure, fire drill, heckler

_____

2. broken water line, oil well, Old Faithful

_____

3. two-year drought, severe illness, serious shortage

_____

4. gag, noose, cough

_____

5. cell, downtown, center of the galaxy

_____

6. old photographs, children, memories

_____

7. tobacco, smoky fire, gasoline

_____

8. sausages, campfires, steaks

_____

9. outcome, results, afterwards

_____

10. warmth, pain, taste buds

_____

Review word: brittle (Lesson 27)

_____   _____   _____

LESSON 29

Read the following selection to get the general meaning. Read it a second time, paying special attention to the words in dark type. Notice how they are used in sentences. These are Master Words. These are the words you will be working with in this lesson.

From **A Christmas Carol**
by Charles Dickens

"Scrooge and Marley's, I believe," said one of the gentlemen, referring to his list. "Have I the pleasure of addressing Mr. Scrooge, or Mr. Marley?"

"Mr. Marley has been dead these seven years," Scrooge replied. "He died seven years ago, this very night."

"We have no doubt his liberality is well represented by his surviving partner," said the gentleman, presenting his **credentials**.

It certainly was; for they had been two **kindred** spirits. At the **ominous** word "liberality," Scrooge frowned, and shook his head, and handed the credentials back.

"At this **festive** season of the year, Mr. Scrooge," said the gentleman, taking up a pen, "it is more than usually desirable that we should make some slight provision for the poor and **destitute**, who suffer greatly at the present time. Many thousands are in want of common necessaries; hundreds of thousands are in want of common comforts, sir."

"Are there no prisons?" asked Scrooge.

"Plenty of prisons," said the gentleman, laying down the pen again.

"And the Union workhouses?" demanded Scrooge. "Are they still in operation?"

"They are. Still," returned the gentleman, "I wish I could say they were not."

"The Treadmill and the Poor Law are in full vigor, then?" said Scrooge.

"Both very busy, sir."

"Oh! I was afraid, from what you said at first, that something had occurred to stop them in their useful course," said Scrooge. "I'm very glad to hear it."

"Under the **impression** that they scarcely furnish Christian cheer of mind or body to the multitude," returned the gentleman, "a few of us are **endeavoring** to raise a fund to buy the Poor some meat and drink, and means of warmth. We choose this time, because it is a time, of all others, when Want is **keenly** felt, and **Abundance** rejoices. What shall I put you down for?"

"Nothing!" Scrooge replied.

"You wish to be **anonymous**?"

"I wish to be left alone," said Scrooge.

EXERCISE 1

SELF-TEST: After reading the above selection, do the following. Look at the Master Words below. Underline the words that you think you know. Circle the words that you are less sure about. Draw a square around the words you don't recognize.

MASTER WORDS

abundance	festive
anonymous	impression
credentials	keen
destitute	kindred
endeavor	ominous

Read the selection on the preceding page again, this time paying special attention to the ten Master Words. In the (a) spaces provided below, write down what you think is the meaning of the word. After you have attempted a definition for each word, look up the word in a dictionary. In the (b) spaces, copy the appropriate dictionary definition.

1. **abundance** (n.)

   a. _____

   b. _____

2. **anonymous** (adj.)

   a. _____

   b. _____

3. **credentials** (n.)

   a. _____

   b. _____

4. **destitute** (n.)

   a. _____

   b. _____

5. **endeavor** (v.)

   a. _____

   b. _____

6. **festive** (adj.)

   a. _____

   b. _____

7. **impression** (n.)

   a. _____

   b. _____

8. **keen** (adj.)

   a. _____

   b. _____

9. **kindred** (adj.)

   a. _____

   b. _____

10. **ominous** (adj.)

   a. _____

   b. _____

EXERCISE 3

Use the following list of synonyms and antonyms to fill in the blanks. Some words have no antonyms. In such cases, the antonym blanks have been marked with an X.

attempt   favorable   merry   plenty   related   threatening
documents   gloomy   nameless   poor   sharp   unconnected
dull   known   opinion   quit   shortage   wealthy

	Synonyms	**Antonyms**
1. **credentials**	_____	X _____
2. **kindred**	_____	_____
3. **ominous**	_____	_____
4. **festive**	_____	_____
5. **destitute**	_____	_____
6. **impression**	_____	X _____
7. **endeavor**	_____	_____
8. **keen**	_____	_____
9. **abundance**	_____	_____
10. **anonymous**	_____	_____

EXERCISE 4

Decide whether the first pair in the items below are synonyms or antonyms. Then choose the Master Word that shows a similar relation to the word(s) preceding the blank.

1. nucleus	:heart	::try	: _____
2. fumes	:vapor	::papers	: _____
3. disrupt	:promote	::deadened	: _____
4. acute	:blunt	::promising	: _____
5. gush	:seep	::unhappy	: _____
6. ensue	:result	::poverty-stricken	: _____
7. sensation	:paralysis	::different	: _____
8. cherish	:scorn	::lack	: _____
9. sizzle	:hiss	::unidentified	: _____
10. strangle	:suffocate	::idea	: _____

The Master Words in this lesson are repeated below. From the Master Words, choose the appropriate word for the blank in each of the following sentences. Write the word in the numbered space provided at the right.

abundance	credentials	endeavor	impression	kindred
anonymous	destitute	festive	keen	ominous

1. Proceeds from the walk-a-thon will go to the ...?... in our community.

1. _____

2. The FBI agent presented his ...?... to prove his identity.

2. _____

3. The paper refuses to publish ...?... letters, and all comments must appear with the writer's name and address.

3. _____

4. Under the ...?... that the world was flat, ancient sailors cautiously avoided what they thought was the edge of the earth.

4. _____

5. Connie ...?...(d, ed) to break the school record in the 100-yard free-style competition.

5. _____

6. New Year's Eve, with party hats and noisemakers, is usually (a, an) ...?... occasion.

6. _____

7. The twins were not only alike in looks; they also had ...?... interests.

7. _____

8. Although no storms had been predicted, the dark clouds that were gathering looked ...?... .

8. _____

9. A deer's ...?... senses help it quickly spot and avoid an enemy.

9. _____

10. The horn of plenty has come to symbolize the ...?... of the harvest.

10. _____

Use at least five Master Words from this lesson to write a scene about one of the following topics. Or create a topic of your own. Write your choice on the blank. Circle the Master Words as you use them.

Possible Topics: The Mysterious Invitation, The Masked Dancers

_____

_____

_____

_____

_____

_____

_____

_____

Read the following selection to get the general meaning. Read it a second time, paying special attention to the words in dark type. Notice how they are used in sentences. These are Master Words. These are the words you will be working with in this lesson.

From the Inaugural Address of
John F. Kennedy (1961)

In your hands, my fellow citizens, more than mine, will rest the final success or failure of our course. Since this country was founded, each generation of Americans has been **summoned** to give **testimony** to its national loyalty. The graves of young Americans who answered the call to service surround the globe.

Now the trumpet summons us again—not as a call to bear arms, though arms we need—not as a call to battle, though embattled we are—but a call to bear the burden of a long twilight struggle, year in and year out "rejoicing in hope, patient in **tribulation**"—a struggle against the common enemies of man: **tyranny**, poverty, disease, and war itself.

Can we **forge** against these enemies a grand and global **alliance**, North and South, East and West, that can assure a more **fruitful** life for all mankind? Will you join in that historic effort?

In the long history of the world, only a few generations have been granted the role of defending freedom in its hour of **maximum** danger. I do not **shrink** from this responsibility—I welcome it. I do not believe that any of us would exchange places with any other people or any other generation. The energy, the faith, and the **devotion** which we bring to this endeavor will light our country and all who serve it—and the glow from that fire can truly light the world.

And so, my fellow Americans: ask not what your country can do for you—ask what you can do for your country.

My fellow citizens of the world: ask not what America will do for you, but what together we can do for the freedom of man.

Finally, whether you are citizens of America or citizens of the world, ask of us here the same high standards of strength and sacrifice which we ask of you. With a good conscience our only sure reward, with history the final judge of our deeds, let us go forth to lead the land we love, asking His blessing and His help, but knowing that here on earth God's work must truly be our own.

EXERCISE 1

SELF-TEST: After reading the above selection, do the following. Look at the Master Words below. Underline the words that you think you know. Circle the words that you are less sure about. Draw a square around the words you don't recognize.

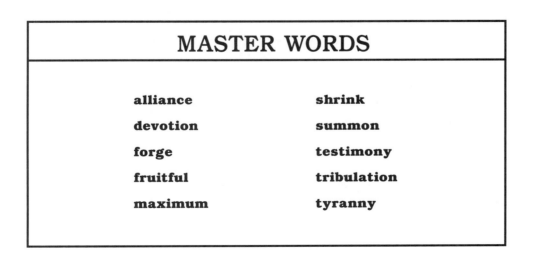

MASTER WORDS

alliance	shrink
devotion	summon
forge	testimony
fruitful	tribulation
maximum	tyranny

Read the selection on the preceding page again, this time paying special attention to the ten Master Words. In the (a) spaces provided below, write down what you think is the meaning of the word. After you have attempted a definition for each word, look up the word in a dictionary. In the (b) spaces, copy the appropriate dictionary definition.

1. **alliance** (n.)

   a. _____

   b. _____

2. **devotion** (n.)

   a. _____

   b. _____

3. **forge** (v.)

   a. _____

   b. _____

4. **fruitful** (adj.)

   a. _____

   b. _____

5. **maximum** (adj.)

   a. _____

   b. _____

6. **shrink** (v.)

   a. _____

   b. _____

7. **summon** (v.)

   a. _____

   b. _____

8. **testimony** (n.)

   a. _____

   b. _____

9. **tribulation** (n.)

   a. _____

   b. _____

10. **tyranny** (n.)

    a. _____

    b. _____

Use the following list of synonyms and antonyms to fill in the blanks. Some words have no antonyms. In such cases, the antonym blanks have been marked with an X.

advance   call   dissolve   form   loyalty   separation
barren   dictatorship   evidence   freedom   minimum   trouble
betrayal   dismiss   flinch   greatest   productive   union
blessing

	Synonyms	**Antonyms**
1. **summon**	_____	_____
2. **testimony**	_____	X
3. **tribulation**	_____	_____
4. **tyranny**	_____	_____
5. **forge**	_____	_____
6. **alliance**	_____	_____
7. **fruitful**	_____	_____
8. **maximum**	_____	_____
9. **shrink**	_____	_____
10. **devotion**	_____	_____

Decide whether the first pair in the items below are synonyms or antonyms. Then choose the Master Word that shows a similar relation to the word(s) preceding the blank.

1. endeavor   :undertake   ::proof   : _____

2. keen   :blunt   ::least   : _____

3. credentials   :certificates   ::partnership   : _____

4. ominous   :hopefulness   ::unfaithfulness   : _____

5. kindred   :alike   ::shape   : _____

6. festive   :cheerless   ::good fortune   : _____

7. anonymous   :unnamed   ::ask for   : _____

8. destitute   :rich   ::independence   : _____

9. abundance   :scarcity   ::approach   : _____

10. impression   :feeling   ::profitable   : _____

The Master Words in this lesson are repeated below. From the Master Words, choose the appropriate word for the blank in each of the following sentences. Write the word in the numbered space provided at the right.

| alliance | forge | maximum | summon | tribulation |
| devotion | fruitful | shrink | testimony | tyranny |

1. According to classical mythology, Vulcan, a gifted metal worker, ...?...(d, ed) Jupiter's thunderbolts deep inside Mt. Etna.

1. _____

2. Often ...?... results when too much power is put in the hands of too few.

2. _____

3. Coach Evans ...?...(d, ed) the team captain to the side of the court for a quick word of advice.

3. _____

4. The great ...?... that man has suffered shows in his haggard face.

4. _____

5. According to the ...?... of the consumer in the commercial, new Super-Brite produced cleaner laundry than Brand X.

5. _____

6. A person who ...?...(s) from the sight of blood has little hope of becoming a surgeon.

6. _____

7. Farmland is generally more ...?... after it has been enriched with minerals.

7. _____

8. Throughout history, nations have tended to form (a, an) ...?... against their common enemies.

8. _____

9. The ...?... number of people allowed into the hall was 5,000; the fire department forbade any more than that.

9. _____

10. Most pet owners expect their animals to show affection and ...?... .

10. _____

Write the Master Word that is associated with each word group below. Then list three things that might be associated with the review word that follows.

1. marriage, fans, dog

_____

2. recoil, cringe, back away from

_____

3. bumper crop, oil gusher, best-selling author

_____

4. United Nations, AFL-CIO, NATO

_____

5. speed limit, high dosage, the most

_____

6. sworn statement, witness, lawyer

_____

7. dinner bell, court order, fire alarm

_____

8. war, plague, Holocaust

_____

9. iron fist, Hitler, dictator

_____

10. sparks, cast, hammer

_____

Review word: festive (Lesson 29)

_____   _____   _____

LESSON 31

Read the following selection to get the general meaning. Read it a second time, paying special attention to the words in dark type. Notice how they are used in sentences. These are Master Words. These are the words you will be working with in this lesson.

From **Robinson Crusoe**
by Daniel Defoe

I gave humble and **hearty** thanks that God had been pleased to discover to me, even that it was possible I might be more happy in this **solitary** condition than I should have been in society, and in all the pleasures of the world; that He could fully make up to me the **deficiencies** of my solitary state and the want of human society, by His presence, and the communications of His **grace** to my soul, supporting, comforting, and encouraging me to depend upon His **providence** here, and hope for His eternal presence hereafter.

Before, as I walked about, either on my hunting, or for viewing the country, . . . my very heart would die within me, to think of the woods, the mountains, the deserts I was in; and how I was a prisoner, locked up with the eternal bolts and bars of the ocean, in an **uninhabited** wilderness, without **redemption**. In the midst of the greatest **composures** of my mind, this would break out upon me like a storm, and make me **wring** my hands, and weep like a child. Sometimes it would take me in the middle of my work, and I would immediately sit down and sigh, and look down upon the ground for an hour or two together; and this was still worse to me; for if I could burst out into tears, or **vent** myself by words, it would go off, and the grief, having exhausted itself, would abate.

EXERCISE 1

SELF-TEST: After reading the above selection, do the following. Look at the Master Words below. Underline the words that you think you know. Circle the words that you are less sure about. Draw a square around the words you don't recognize.

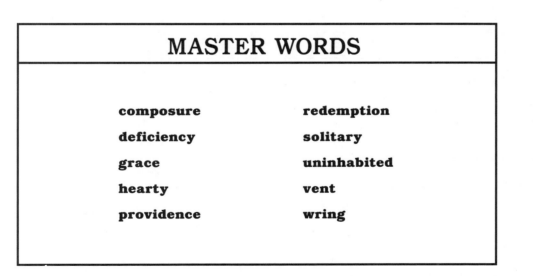

MASTER WORDS

composure	redemption
deficiency	solitary
grace	uninhabited
hearty	vent
providence	wring

Read the selection on the preceding page again, this time paying special attention to the ten Master Words. In the (a) spaces provided below, write down what you think is the meaning of the word. After you have attempted a definition for each word, look up the word in a dictionary. In the (b) spaces, copy the appropriate dictionary definition.

1. **composure** (n.)

    a. _____

    b. _____

2. **deficiency** (n.)

    a. _____

    b. _____

3. **grace** (n.)

    a. _____

    b. _____

4. **hearty** (adj.)

    a. _____

    b. _____

5. **providence** (n.)

    a. _____

    b. _____

6. **redemption** (n.)

    a. _____

    b. _____

7. **solitary** (adj.)

    a. _____

    b. _____

8. **uninhabited** (adj.)

    a. _____

    b. _____

9. **vent** (v.)

    a. _____

    b. _____

10. **wring** (v.)

    a. _____

    b. _____

Use the following list of synonyms and antonyms to fill in the blanks. Some words have no antonyms. In such cases, the antonym blanks have been marked with an X.

abundance	alone	divine care	populated	shortage	suppress
accompanied	calmness	lukewarm	release	sin	twist
agitation	damnation	mercy	salvation	sincere	unoccupied

	Synonyms	**Antonyms**
1. **hearty**	_____	_____
2. **solitary**	_____	_____
3. **deficiency**	_____	_____
4. **grace**	_____	_____
5. **providence**	_____	X
6. **uninhabited**	_____	_____
7. **redemption**	_____	_____
8. **composure**	_____	_____
9. **wring**	_____	X
10. **vent**	_____	_____

Decide whether the first pair in the items below are synonyms or antonyms. Then choose the Master Word that shows a similar relation to the word(s) preceding the blank.

1. testimony	:sworn statement	::God's care	: _____
2. alliance	:bond	::let out	: _____
3. maximum	:lowest	::nervousness	: _____
4. devotion	:double-crossing	::occupied	: _____
5. tribulation	:woe	::genuine	: _____
6. forge	:mold	::squeeze	: _____
7. tyranny	:total power	::isolated	: _____
8. summon	:call for	::forgiveness	: _____
9. fruitful	:worthless	::doom	: _____
10. shrink	:face	::surplus	: _____

The Master Words in this lesson are repeated below. From the Master Words, choose the appropriate word for the blank in each of the following sentences. Write the word in the numbered space provided at the right.

| composure | grace | providence | solitary | vent |
| deficiency | hearty | redemption | uninhabited | wring |

1. Although the book was due on Monday, the librarian allowed two days of ...?... before making me pay a fine.

1. _____

2. When asked an embarrassing question, the president briefly lost his ...?... .

2. _____

3. Eating fruits and vegetables may prevent a vitamin ...?... .

3. _____

4. Because Mother did not ...?... her grief when her sister died, she spent months recovering from her loss.

4. _____

5. The tag on the drip-dry garment warned, "Do not ...?... ."

5. _____

6. Jean's parents gave warm, ...?... approval to her decision to be a journalist.

6. _____

7. Hermits seek (a, an) ...?... life, but most of us are happier when friends and family are close by.

7. _____

8. Thanks to ...?..., we had been able to make the 300-mile trip through the blizzard without any serious accident.

8. _____

9. The minister said that complete ...?... is possible for the worst sinner if he or she truly repents.

9. _____

10. After searching the island for three days without finding a soul, I realized the place was ...?... .

10. _____

Order the words in each item from *least* to *most*. Use the abbreviations *L* for "least" and *M* for "most." Leave the line before the word of the middle degree blank. The first word provides a clue about how to arrange the words. See the example.

elegant: __M__stately   __L__crude   ____modest

(*Crude* indicates the least elegant; *stately* indicates the most elegant.)

1. settled: ____uninhabited   ____urbanized   ____colonized

2. lacking: ____deficiency   ____absence   ____abundance

3. crowded: ____jam-packed   ____solitary   ____few

4. troubled: ____composure   ____hysteria   ____nervous

5. fast-drying: ____blow dry   ____wring   ____drip dry

6. eruption: ____vent   ____burst   ____bottle up

7. mercy: ____grace   ____cruelty   ____concern

8. saved: ____recovery   ____redemption   ____loss

9. friendly: ____hearty   ____cold   ____polite

10. trusted: ____luck   ____providence   ____traitor

Read the following selection to get the general meaning. Read it a second time, paying special attention to the words in dark type. Notice how they are used in sentences. These are Master Words. These are the words you will be working with in this lesson.

From "The Revolt of Mother"
by Mary E. Wilkins Freeman

Nanny and Sammy stared at each other. There was something strange in their mother's manner. Mrs. Penn did not eat anything herself. She went into the **pantry**, and they heard her moving dishes while they ate. **Presently** she came out with a pile of plates. She got the clothes-basket out of the shed, and packed them in it. Nanny and Sammy watched. She brought out cups and saucers and put them in with the plates.

"What you goin' to do, mother?" inquired Nanny, in a **timid** voice. A sense of something unusual made her tremble, as if it were a ghost. Sammy rolled his eyes over his pie.

"You'll see what I'm goin' to do," replied Mrs. Penn. "If you're through, Nanny, I want you to go upstairs an' pack up your things; an' I want you, Sammy, to help me take down the bed in the bedroom."

"Oh, mother, what for?" gasped Nanny.

"You'll see."

During the next few hours a **feat** was performed by this simple, **pious** New England mother which was equal in its way to Wolfe's storming of the Heights of Abraham. It took no more **genius** and **audacity** of bravery for Wolfe to cheer his wondering soldiers up those steep **precipices**, under the sleeping eyes of the enemy, than for Sarah Penn, at the head of her children, to move all their little household goods into the new barn while her husband was away.

Nanny and Sammy followed their mother's instructions without a murmur; indeed, they were overawed. There is a certain **uncanny** and superhuman quality about all such purely original **undertakings** as their mother's was to them. Nanny went back and forth with her light loads, and Sammy tugged with sober energy.

At five o'clock in the afternoon the little house in which the Penns had lived for forty years had emptied itself into the new barn.

EXERCISE 1

SELF-TEST: After reading the above selection, do the following. Look at the Master Words below. Underline the words that you think you know. Circle the words that you are less sure about. Draw a square around the words you don't recognize.

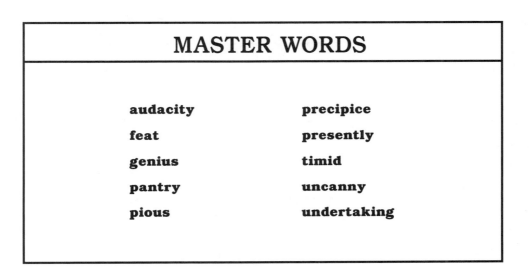

MASTER WORDS

audacity	**precipice**
feat	**presently**
genius	**timid**
pantry	**uncanny**
pious	**undertaking**

Read the selection on the preceding page again, this time paying special attention to the ten Master Words. In the (a) spaces provided below, write down what you think is the meaning of the word. After you have attempted a definition for each word, look up the word in a dictionary. In the (b) spaces, copy the appropriate dictionary definition.

1. **audacity** (n.)

    a. _____

    b. _____

2. **feat** (n.)

    a. _____

    b. _____

3. **genius** (n.)

    a. _____

    b. _____

4. **pantry** (n.)

    a. _____

    b. _____

5. **pious** (adj.)

    a. _____

    b. _____

6. **precipice** (n.)

    a. _____

    b. _____

7. **presently** (adv.)

    a. _____

    b. _____

8. **timid** (adj.)

    a. _____

    b. _____

9. **uncanny** (adj.)

    a. _____

    b. _____

10. **undertaking** (n.)

    a. _____

    b. _____

Use the following list of synonyms and antonyms to fill in the blanks. Some words have no antonyms. In such cases, the antonym blanks have been marked with an X.

achievement	incompetence	meekness	project	shy	talent
bold	irreverent	ordinary	recklessness	soon	weird
cliff	later	plateau	religious	storeroom	

	Synonyms	**Antonyms**
1. **pantry**	_____	X
2. **presently**	_____	_____
3. **timid**	_____	_____
4. **feat**	_____	X
5. **pious**	_____	_____
6. **genius**	_____	_____
7. **audacity**	_____	_____
8. **precipice**	_____	_____
9. **uncanny**	_____	_____
10. **undertaking**	_____	X

Decide whether the first pair in the items below are synonyms or antonyms. Then choose the Master Word that shows a similar relation to the word(s) preceding the blank.

1. providence	:heavenly protection	::ledge	: _____
2. composure	:uproar	::caution	: _____
3. vent	:pour out	::task	: _____
4. uninhabited	:settled	::brash	: _____
5. wring	:twist	::cupboard	: _____
6. grace	:disfavor	::afterward	: _____
7. hearty	:indifferent	::unholy	: _____
8. solitary	:escorted	::natural	: _____
9. redemption	:saving	::accomplishment	: _____
10. deficiency	:overload	::unskillfulness	: _____

The Master Words in this lesson are repeated below. From the Master Words, choose the appropriate word for the blank in each of the following sentences. Write the word in the numbered space provided at the right.

audacity	genius	pious	presently	uncanny
feat	pantry	precipice	timid	undertaking

1. We kept canned goods, cleaning supplies, and pans in the ...?... .

1. _____

2. Although he had (a, an) ...?... for physics, Albert Einstein supposedly failed algebra repeatedly.

2. _____

3. The secretary invited me to sit down and said that Mrs. Walker would see me ...?... .

3. _____

4. Handbills for Marvel the Magician promised wonderful ...?...(s) of magic.

4. _____

5. Teachers seem to have (a, an) ...?... ability to know what is going on behind their backs.

5. _____

6. Along the coast of Cornwall are many beautiful but treacherous ...?...(s) which overlook the sea.

6. _____

7. Whenever strangers were around, the ...?... child hid behind her mother.

7. _____

8. Building a new swimming pool proved to be a greater ...?... than the townspeople had expected.

8. _____

9. The ...?... man said his prayers daily and respected the holy men.

9. _____

10. Bart had the ...?... to ask for a day off just after he had been absent for an entire week.

10. _____

Fill in the chart below with the Master Word that fits each set of clues. Part of speech refers to the word's usage in the lesson. Use a dictionary when necessary.

Number of Syllables	Part of Speech	Other Clues	Master Word
2	adjective	appropriate name for a pope	1. _____
4	noun	a report or project, for instance	2. _____
1	noun	one of these takes bravery and skill	3. _____
3	adverb	when you hope to be paid	4. _____
2	noun	you might raid this when hungry	5. _____
4	noun	"guts" or "nerve"	6. _____
2	adjective	mice are said to be this way	7. _____
3	adjective	when the door opens and closes by itself, for instance	8. _____
2	noun	some say Shakespeare had this	9. _____
3	noun	challenge for a mountain climber	10. _____

Read the following selection to get the general meaning. Read it a second time, paying special attention to the words in dark type. Notice how they are used in sentences. These are Master Words. These are the words you will be working with in this lesson.

From **The Nitty Gritty**
by Frank Bonham

Woodson swung the Cadillac down an off ramp into a downtown area. The buildings were all old and **dingy**. He slowed at an intersection. On one corner, Charlie saw a large brick church, on another, a gas station, and next to the gas station a two-story wooden **structure** that occupied a full half-block. A neon sign on the roof glowed in the night.

BALBOA **HIPPODROME**

As Woodson parked in front, a young man standing near the box office hurried to the curb. Woodson stepped out but told the boys to stay in the car.

"How's the **gate**?" he asked the man, who wore a uniform with BALBOA HIPPODROME stitched on the back.

"Pretty good, Mr. Woodson."

"Take these boys around to the side entrance. Show them to the dressing room after you park the car."

Charlie began questioning the **attendant** as soon as he drove into the alley beside the building. "What do we have to do? We aren't really boxers, man—"

The man smiled. "You'll fight with gloves as big as pillows, and just kind of mash each other around. You'll have as much fun as anybody, and if you really put on a good show, they'll throw money at you. Nothing to it."

He led them through a side door of the barny old building into a dimly-lit hall that smelled like a vacuum cleaner bag full of **stale** popcorn. The wooden walls, ceiling and floor looked so dry that Charlie figured if you dropped a match the whole works would go off like a firecracker. **Evidently** the Fire Department thought so, too, because there was a fire **extinguisher** every few yards and *Exit* signs and arrows at every turn.

They came to an open door and the attendant walked inside. Charlie stepped timidly after him into a large room with **battered** metal lockers lining the walls. There was a toilet in an **alcove**, a number of benches where men in boxing trunks and robes sat or lay resting, some scales, and a washbowl. Bolted to the wall was a metal box with a red cross on it and the words "First Aid."

"Take a locker and make yourselves comfortable," said the attendant. "Mr. Woodson will tell you when you go on."

—The Nitty Gritty *by Frank Bonham.*
Copyright 1968 by Frank Bonham. E. P. Dutton & Co., Publishers.

EXERCISE 1

SELF-TEST: After reading the above selection, do the following. Look at the Master Words below. Underline the words that you think you know. Circle the words that you are less sure about. Draw a square around the words you don't recognize.

MASTER WORDS

alcove	**evident**	**hippodrome**
attendant	**extinguisher**	**stale**
batter	**gate**	**structure**
dingy		

Read the selection on the preceding page again, this time paying special attention to the ten Master Words. In the (a) spaces provided below, write down what you think is the meaning of the word. After you have attempted a definition for each word, look up the word in a dictionary. In the (b) spaces, copy the appropriate dictionary definition.

1. **alcove** (n.)

    a. _____

    b. _____

2. **attendant** (n.)

    a. _____

    b. _____

3. **batter** (v.)

    a. _____

    b. _____

4. **dingy** (adj.)

    a. _____

    b. _____

5. **evident** (adj.)

    a. _____

    b. _____

6. **extinguisher** (n.)

    a. _____

    b. _____

7. **gate** (n.)

    a. _____

    b. _____

8. **hippodrome** (n.)

    a. _____

    b. _____

9. **stale** (adj.)

    a. _____

    b. _____

10. **structure** (n.)

    a. _____

    b. _____

Use the following list of synonyms and antonyms to fill in the blanks. Some words have no antonyms. In such cases, the antonym blanks have been marked with an X.

apparent	building	fuse	nook	repair
arena	drab	helper	old	sprinkler
beat	fresh	manager	receipts	veiled
bright				

	Synonyms	**Antonyms**
1. **dingy**	_____	_____
2. **structure**	_____	X
3. **hippodrome**	_____	X
4. **gate**	_____	X
5. **attendant**	_____	_____
6. **stale**	_____	_____
7. **evident**	_____	_____
8. **extinguisher**	_____	_____
9. **batter**	_____	_____
10. **alcove**	_____	X

Decide whether the first pair in the items below are synonyms or antonyms. Then choose the Master Word that shows a similar relation to the word(s) preceding the blank.

1. precipice	:bluff	::servant	: _____
2. audacity	:shyness	::unclear	: _____
3. timid	:daring	::starter	: _____
4. pious	:sinful	::new	: _____
5. undertaking	:effort	::corner	: _____
6. uncanny	:normal	::fix up	: _____
7. pantry	:storage closet	::admissions	: _____
8. presently	:shortly	::stadium	: _____
9. genius	:incapability	::shining	: _____
10. feat	:deed	::shelter	: _____

EXERCISE 5

The Master Words in this lesson are repeated below. From the Master Words, choose the appropriate word for the blank in each of the following sentences. Write the word in the numbered space provided at the right.

| alcove | batter | evident | gate | stale |
| attendant | dingy | extinguisher | hippodrome | structure |

1. The sunny ...?... on the east side of the kitchen made an ideal breakfast nook.

1. _____

2. "It is ...?... that you have the chicken pox," Dr. Wilson declared after only a glance at his patient.

2. _____

3. After several years the couch had (a, an) ...?... appearance; areas that should have been cream-colored appeared gray.

3. _____

4. The ...?... for the rock concert set a new record for the auditorium.

4. _____

5. As a spark in the lab ignited some papers, Matt raced for the fire ...?... .

5. _____

6. The Washington Monument, a hollow ...?..., contains 189 carved stones from around the world presented by admirers of George Washington.

6. _____

7. The ...?... at the parking garage worked the night shift.

7. _____

8. If we keep a loaf of bread too long and it grows ...?..., Dad will feed it to the birds.

8. _____

9. The attackers tried to ...?... down the castle gate with a huge log.

9. _____

10. A three-ring circus was scheduled to appear at the ...?... during the first week of June.

10. _____

EXERCISE 6

The invented words below are formed from parts of different Master Words from this lesson. Create a definition and indicate the part of speech for each word. The first one is done for you.

stalegate   *(n.) an audience made up of repeat attenders* _____

hippodrattendant _____

stalingy _____

structurbatter _____

Now invent your own words by combining parts of the Master Words. Create a definition for each, and indicate the word's part of speech. (You may reuse any of the word parts above in new combinations.)

1. _____   _____

2. _____   _____

LESSON 34

Read the following selection to get the general meaning. Read it a second time, paying special attention to the words in dark type. Notice how they are used in sentences. These are Master Words. These are the words you will be working with in this lesson.

From "The Bishop's Candlesticks"
by Victor Hugo

As the cathedral clock struck two, Jean Valjean awoke. What awakened him was that it was too good a bed. For nineteen years he had not slept in a bed, and his sleep was unquiet.

Many thoughts came to him as he lay there, but one repeated itself and drove away all others. For he remembered the six silver plates and the large silver **ladle** that he had seen Mme. Magloire putting away in the cupboard, and the thought of them took possession of him. There they were, a few steps away. They were solid, and old silver; they would bring at least two hundred francs, double what he had earned in those long years of imprisonment.

His mind struggled with this thought for an hour, when the clock struck three. He opened his eyes, **thrust** out his legs, placed his feet on the ground, and sat on the edge of the bed, lost in thought. He might have remained there until daybreak, if the clock had not struck the quarter-hour. It seemed to say to him, "Come along!"

He rose to his feet, hesitated for a moment, and listened. All was still. He walked **cautiously** toward the window; it had no bars, opened into the garden, and was unfastened. The garden was **enclosed** with a low white wall that he could easily **scale**.

He turned quickly, like a man with mind made up, went to the alcove, where he took his pack, put his shoes into a pocket, swung his bundle upon his shoulders, put on his cap, and pulled it down over his eyes. Holding his breath, he moved toward the door of the bishop's room with **stealthy** steps. There was not a sound.

Jean Valjean pushed open the door.

A deep calm filled the **chamber**. At the further end of the room he could hear the quiet breathing of the sleeping bishop. A ray of moonlight, coming through the high window, suddenly lighted up the bishop's pale face. He slept **tranquilly**. His head had fallen on the pillow in an attitude of untroubled slumber; over the side of the bed hung his hand, **ornamented** with the pastoral ring. His countenance was lit with an expression of hope and happiness.

For a moment Jean Valjean did not remove his eyes from the face of the old man. Then he walked quickly along the bed straight to the cupboard at its head; the key was in it; he opened it and took the basket of silver, crossed the room with **hasty** stride, stepped out the window, put the silver in his knapsack, threw away the basket, ran across the garden, leaped over the wall like a tiger, and fled.

EXERCISE 1

SELF-TEST: After reading the above selection, do the following. Look at the Master Words below. Underline the words that you think you know. Circle the words that you are less sure about. Draw a square around the words you don't recognize.

MASTER WORDS

cautious	ladle	stealthy
chamber	ornament	thrust
enclose	scale	tranquil
hasty		

Read the selection on the preceding page again, this time paying special attention to the ten Master Words. In the (a) spaces provided below, write down what you think is the meaning of the word. After you have attempted a definition for each word, look up the word in a dictionary. In the (b) spaces, copy the appropriate dictionary definition.

1. **cautious** (adj.)

   a. _____

   b. _____

2. **chamber** (n.)

   a. _____

   b. _____

3. **enclose** (v.)

   a. _____

   b. _____

4. **hasty** (adj.)

   a. _____

   b. _____

5. **ladle** (n.)

   a. _____

   b. _____

6. **ornament** (v.)

   a. _____

   b. _____

7. **scale** (v.)

   a. _____

   b. _____

8. **stealthy** (adj.)

   a. _____

   b. _____

9. **thrust** (v.)

   a. _____

   b. _____

10. **tranquil** (adj.)

   a. _____

   b. _____

Use the following list of synonyms and antonyms to fill in the blanks. Some words have no antonyms. In such cases, the antonym blanks have been marked with an X.

adorn	careful	descend	leisurely	room	straightforward
agitated	careless	dipper	pull	secretive	surround
calm	climb	hurried	push	spoil	

	Synonyms	**Antonyms**
1. **ladle**	_____	X _____
2. **thrust**	_____	_____
3. **cautious**	_____	_____
4. **enclose**	_____	X _____
5. **scale**	_____	_____
6. **stealthy**	_____	_____
7. **chamber**	_____	X _____
8. **tranquil**	_____	_____
9. **ornament**	_____	_____
10. **hasty**	_____	_____

Decide whether the first pair in the items below are synonyms or antonyms. Then choose the Master Word that shows a similar relation to the word(s) preceding the blank.

1. evident	:hidden	::tug	: _____
2. attendant	:assistant	::bedroom	: _____
3. extinguisher	:lighter	::reckless	: _____
4. alcove	:cubbyhole	::fence	: _____
5. gate	:income	::ascend	: _____
6. hippodrome	:coliseum	::spoon	: _____
7. stale	:latest	::restless	: _____
8. batter	:mend	::slow	: _____
9. dingy	:gleaming	::open	: _____
10. structure	:building	::decorate	: _____

The Master Words in this lesson are repeated below. From the Master Words, choose the appropriate word for the blank in each of the following sentences. Write the word in the numbered space provided at the right.

cautious	enclose	ladle	scale	thrust
chamber	hasty	ornament	stealthy	tranquil

1. Three marble vases ...?...(d, ed) the top of the mantlepiece.

1. _____

2. A six-foot fence ...?...(d, ed) the yard so that the dog could not escape into the neighborhood.

2. _____

3. Aunt Agatha retired to her ...?... each evening at precisely nine o'clock and didn't come out again until breakfast.

3. _____

4. The ...?... cat burglar crept into the room and quietly picked up the jewelry box.

4. _____

5. Pete would not serve the soup until he found grandmother's silver ...?... .

5. _____

6. Because time for the test was nearly up, Julie could scribble only (a, an) ...?... answer to the last question.

6. _____

7. Sir Edmund Hillary and a Nepalese tribesman were the first to ...?... Mt. Everest, the highest mountain in the world.

7. _____

8. With one quick ...?... of his rapier, the Italian wounded his foe.

8. _____

9. (A, An) ...?... driver always signals a turn even when no other car is apparently in sight.

9. _____

10. When Carla realized that her project would be completed on schedule, (a, an) ...?... feeling came over her.

10. _____

To complete this puzzle, fill in the Master Word associated with each phrase below. Then unscramble the circled letters to form a Master Word from Lesson 33, and define it.

1. to fence in

2. be this way when you approach a traffic light

3. speedy

4. one way to get on top of a wall

5. a spy may act in this manner

6. a lake without a ripple

7. forceful way to open a door

8. fancy term for a bedroom

9. to put up holiday lights, for instance

10. a spoon for gravy or soup

Unscrambled word: _____

Definition: _____

Read the following selection to get the general meaning. Read it a second time, paying special attention to the words in dark type. Notice how they are used in sentences. These are Master Words. These are the words you will be working with in this lesson.

Spoken by Chief Seattle to Governor Stevens of Washington Territory (1854)

It matters little where we pass the **remnant** of our days. They will not be many. A few more moons; a few more winters—and not one of the **descendants** of the mighty hosts that once moved over this broad land or lived in happy homes, protected by the Great Spirit, will remain to **mourn** over the graves of a people once more powerful and hopeful than yours. But why should I mourn at the **untimely** fate of my people? Tribe follows tribe, and nation follows nation, like the waves of the sea. It is the order of nature, and regret is useless. Your time of decay may be distant, but it will surely come, for even the White Man whose God walked and talked with him as friend with friend, cannot be **exempt** from the common destiny. We may be brothers after all. We will see . . . .

Every part of this soil is sacred in the **estimation** of my people. Every hillside, every valley, every plain and grove, has been **hallowed** by some sad or happy event in days long vanished. The very dust upon which you now stand responds more lovingly to their footsteps than to yours, because it is rich with the blood of our ancestors, and our bare feet are conscious of the sympathetic touch. Even the little children who lived here and rejoiced here for a brief season will love these **somber** solitudes and at eventide they greet shadowy returning spirits. And when the last Red Man shall have perished, and the memory of my tribe shall have become a **myth** among the White Men, these shores will swarm with the invisible dead of my tribe, and when your children's children think themselves alone in the field, the store, the shop, upon the highway, or in the silence of the pathless woods, they will not be alone. At night when the streets of your cities and villages are silent and you think them deserted, they will **throng** with the returning hosts that once filled and still love this beautiful land. The White Man will never be alone.

Let him be just and deal kindly with my people, for the dead are not powerless. Dead, did I say? There is no death, only a change of worlds.

—From The Portable North American Indian Reader, F.W. Turner III, ed. Copyright 1973, 1974 by The Viking Press, Inc. Reprinted by permission of The Viking Press.

EXERCISE 1

SELF-TEST: After reading the above selection, do the following. Look at the Master Words below. Underline the words that you think you know. Circle the words that you are less sure about. Draw a square around the words you don't recognize.

MASTER WORDS

descendant	myth
estimation	remnant
exempt	somber
hallow	throng
mourn	untimely

Read the selection on the preceding page again, this time paying special attention to the ten Master Words. In the (a) spaces provided below, write down what you think is the meaning of the word. After you have attempted a definition for each word, look up the word in a dictionary. In the (b) spaces, copy the appropriate dictionary definition.

1. **descendant** (n.)

    a. _____

    b. _____

2. **estimation** (n.)

    a. _____

    b. _____

3. **exempt** (adj.)

    a. _____

    b. _____

4. **hallow** (v.)

    a. _____

    b. _____

5. **mourn** (v.)

    a. _____

    b. _____

6. **myth** (n.)

    a. _____

    b. _____

7. **remnant** (n.)

    a. _____

    b. _____

8. **somber** (adj.)

    a. _____

    b. _____

9. **throng** (v.)

    a. _____

    b. _____

10. **untimely** (adj.)

    a. _____

    b. _____

Use the following list of synonyms and antonyms to fill in the blanks. Some words have no antonyms. In such cases, the antonym blanks have been marked with an X.

ancestor	disperse	gloomy	legend	pollute	seasonable
bless	early	grieve	offspring	rejoice	swarm
bright	excused	leftover	opinion	required	whole
certainty	fact				

	Synonyms	**Antonyms**
1. **remnant**	_____	_____
2. **descendant**	_____	_____
3. **mourn**	_____	_____
4. **untimely**	_____	_____
5. **exempt**	_____	_____
6. **estimation**	_____	_____
7. **hallow**	_____	_____
8. **somber**	_____	_____
9. **myth**	_____	_____
10. **throng**	_____	_____

Decide whether the first pair in the items below are synonyms or antonyms. Then choose the Master Word that shows a similar relation to the word(s) preceding the blank.

1. chamber	:room	::remainder	: _____
2. enclose	:encircle	::crowd	: _____
3. thrust	:shove	::make holy	: _____
4. cautious	:daring	::cheerful	: _____
5. scale	:climb down	::true story	: _____
6. ladle	:scoop	::judgment	: _____
7. ornament	:beautify	::child	: _____
8. tranquil	:disturbed	::opportune	: _____
9. hasty	:unhurried	::celebrate	: _____
10. stealthy	:unhidden	::included	: _____

EXERCISE 5

The Master Words in this lesson are repeated below. From the Master Words, choose the appropriate word for the blank in each of the following sentences. Write the word in the numbered space provided at the right.

descendant	exempt	mourn	remnant	throng
estimation	hallow	myth	somber	untimely

1. A huge crowd ...?...(ed) to catch a glimpse of the President as he rode through the streets.

1. _____

2. I made a quilt from ...?...(s) of material I'd used in other projects.

2. _____

3. People generally dress in ...?... clothes for a funeral.

3. _____

4. Since the rest of the family was discussing her birthday gift, Erica's entrance proved to be ...?... .

4. _____

5. The priests sprinkled the floor with holy water and chanted sacred verse to ...?... the new temple.

5. _____

6. In the ...?... of many critics, Eugene O'Neill and Tennessee Williams are the greatest playwrights America has produced.

6. _____

7. David traced his family tree and discovered he was (a, an) ...?... of King James.

7. _____

8. Because of his broken leg, Josh will be ...?... from physical education class for over three months.

8. _____

9. Martha ...?...(ed) the loss of her cat for several days.

9. _____

10. According to a Greek ...?..., Medusa had hair made out of snakes, and she could turn people into stone.

10. _____

EXERCISE 6

Write the Master Word that is associated with each word group below. Then list three things that might be associated with the review word that follows.

1. shrine, saint, sanctuary

_____

2. family tree, grandchild, future generations

_____

3. loss, death, parting

_____

4. overcast sky, frown, bad news

_____

5. square of carpet, relic, bit of cloth

_____

6. Grand Central Station, traffic jam, swarm

_____

7. immune, underage, tax-free

_____

8. sudden illness, unwanted interruption, premature birth

_____

9. Thor, Hercules, Zeus

_____

10. viewpoint, opinion poll, letter of reference

_____

Review word: scale (Lesson 34)

_____   _____   _____

LESSON 36

PART I: From the list below, choose the appropriate word for each sentence that follows. Use each word only once. There will be two words left over.

abundance	exempt	resentful	superior	undertaking
alliance	impression	strategy	tyranny	untimely
disrupt	overwhelm	summon	uncanny	

1. Everyone marveled at the _____ ability of the mind reader to answer correctly the most intimate questions.

2. A winter storm _____(d, ed) power service in the downtown area for three hours.

3. During a time of plenty, wise people set aside a portion of the _____ for that rainy day certain to come along.

4. The _____ death of Stephen Crane at twenty-nine no doubt deprived the world of brilliant short stories, novels, and poetry.

5. The project will be a major _____, costing billions of dollars and taking ten years to complete.

6. The city council decided that seniors would be _____ from the curfew rule on the night of the prom.

7. The two nations formed (a, an) _____, agreeing to fight together when their hostile neighbor threatened to attack.

8. Under the _____ that her guest did not eat meat, Mrs. Simmons prepared a lunch of vegetables, bread, and fruit.

9. With two term papers and three finals still to face, Anna felt _____(d, ed) by her workload.

10. In order that consumers might enjoy _____ flavor, most packages of food are stamped with a "freshness" date.

11. In countries where _____ exists, people do not dare to criticize their ruler.

12. Marty is spoiled and becomes _____ when he doesn't get his way.

PART II: Decide whether the first pair in the items below are synonyms or antonyms. Then choose a Master Word from Lessons 25-35 which shows a similar relation to the word(s) preceding the blank. Do not repeat a Master Word that appears in the first column.

1. conduct   :guide   ::treasure   : _____

2. destitute   :well-to-do   ::usual   : _____

3. keen   :piercing   ::quick   : _____

4. fruitful   :unproductive   ::uncaring   : _____

5. audacity   :daring   ::delicate   : _____

PART III: From the list below, choose the appropriate word for each sentence that follows. Use each word only once. There will be three words left over.

alcove	commendable	feat	maximum	testimony
annihilation	credentials	fumes	ponder	tranquil
betray	deficiency	hasty	profound	uninhabited

1. Carbon monoxide _____ —both colorless and odorless—are among the most deadly to humans.

2. The _____ of the witness seemed to support the defendant's story.

3. A sign in the front of the bus stated that the _____ number of passengers the bus could carry was sixty.

4. Griff hoped that by attending summer school he would be able to make up his _____ of math credits.

5. Although most people thought the old house was _____, we had seen mysterious shadows move down the creaky staircase.

6. Landing the Viking spacecraft on Mars was (a, an) _____ requiring years of scientific study by people from many nations.

7. By putting shelves in (a, an) _____, Bev turned a corner of her room into a pleasant private library.

8. Law officers usually carry _____ to prove their identity unless they are working undercover.

9. At the community theater, Sheila gave (a, an) _____ performance as Anne Frank which won her a standing ovation.

10. Shakespeare's _____ insight into human nature has made his plays appealing for all types of people and all generations.

11. Which is the greater crime: to prove false to a friend or to _____ one's country?

12. Though the owners pressed Mario for a snap decision about buying their house, he wanted time to _____ his answer.

PART IV: Decide whether the first pair in the items below are synonyms or antonyms. Then choose a Master Word from Lessons 25-35 which shows a similar relation to the word(s) preceding the blank. Do not repeat a Master Word that appears in the first column.

1. tranquil   :unsettled   ::edge   : _____

2. smolder   :flare up   ::make merry   : _____

3. enlighten   :mix up   ::bright   : _____

4. ominous   :menacing   ::unattended   : _____

5. composure   :calmness   ::grasp   : _____

INDEX — Word and Lesson Number

J

just, 14

K

keen, 29
keynote, 19
kindred, 29
knead, 19

L

ladle, 34
lash (n), 3
lash (v), 10
lean, 26
liberality, 21
loom, 17
lyrics, 19

M

maximum, 30
meddle, 1
merely, 13
mess, 20
metallic, 22
misfortune, 14
mourn, 35
myth, 35

N

nerve, 15
nucleus, 28
numb, 5

O

ominous, 29
onlooking, 22
ornament, 34
overtake, 14
overwhelm, 26

P

panorama, 17
pantry, 32
particle, 1
passion, 8
passport, 3
peculiar, 15
peer, 26

perish, 18
picturesque, 17
pious, 32
pitiable, 7
plank, 3
podium, 19
ponder, 26
porcelain, 9
precipice, 32
presently, 32
prey, 18
prime, 4
profess, 23
profit, 22
profound, 26
prolong, 1
prompt, 8
propitious, 17
propose, 21
prospect, 18
prosperous, 16
providence, 31
provision, 18

Q

quarter, 23
Quonset, 9

R

rapier, 26
ravenous, 18
receptive, 16
recollection, 9
recommend, 23
redemption, 31
reel, 25
refer, 13
reflect, 13
refuge, 3
regiment, 13
regulation, 20
relationship, 9
relative, 15
remnant, 35
repentant, 3
reproach, 14
resentful, 26
resistant, 9
resolution, 10
respects, 25
rile, 2

S

saddle, 11
sagacious, 27
salvation, 3
scale, 34
seize, 25
sensation, 28
sensitivity, 19
sentinel, 20
sheath, 5
shrill, 16
shrink, 30
sizzle, 28
skiff, 10
slant, 10
slay, 1
smolder, 26
snarl, 22
snug, 16
sober, 8
solitary, 31
somber, 35
soothing, 7
spatter, 7
sprawl, 2
sprig, 9
spy, 16
stale, 33
stammer, 25
startling, 8
statement, 15
stealthy, 34
stimulate, 6
strangle, 28
strategy, 27
structure, 33
sublime, 8
subtle, 15
suburban, 9
succession, 20
summon, 30
superb, 17
superior, 27
surround, 22
sustenance, 18
swagger, 2
swarm, 17
synthetic, 9

T

tangle, 8
temper, 1

terms, 11
testimony, 30
theory, 20
throng, 35
thrust, 34
timid, 32
tormentor, 2
touching, 4
trace, 23
trademark, 2
tranquil, 34
transmit, 20
tribulation, 30
troops, 13
tyranny, 30

U

uncanny, 32
undertake, 11
undertaking, 32
uninhabited, 31
unrestrained, 20
untimely, 35
utter, 1

V

vehicle, 7
veil, 25
vent, 31
ventilator, 15
version, 6
vicarious, 22
vice, 2
victim, 22
voluble, 21

W

warrant, 17
waver, 10
wickedness, 14
wring, 31

Y

yelp, 22